Ascendent =
Midheaven =

the *Astrology* of *Sexuality*

Sun conj.   Mars
③   "   Sextile Uranus
    "   opposite Ascendant
Moon trine Jupiter
③ Moon Sq. Saturn
  Moon Sq. Midheaven
Merc. Sex. Venus
   "   "   Saturn
⑤ "   Conj. Neptune
   "   Sex. Pluto
   "   "   Midheaven
Venus Sq. Jupiter
   "   Trine Saturn
⑤ "   Sex. Neptune
   "   Conj. Pluto
④ "   Trine Midth.
② Mars Sextile Sat.
  Mars "   Uranus
① Jupiter Sq. Pluto
Saturn Sex Neptune
② "   Trine Pluto
   "   Conj. Midth
① Uran. Trine Ascend.

② Nept Sex Pluto
   "   Sex Mid.
① Pluto Trine Mid.

Conj = 4
Sex = 11
Opp. = 1
Trine = 6
Square = 4
─────
26

the Astrology of Sexuality

MARTIN SCHULMAN

SAMUEL WEISER, INC.

York Beach, Maine

First published in 1982 by
Samuel Weiser, Inc.
Box 612
York Beach, Maine 03910

Fifth printing, 1992

Library of Congress Catalog Card Number: 82-159118

ISBN 0-87728-481-4
MV

Cover painting:
Hesperus by Sir Joseph Noel-Paton (1821-1901)
Glasgow Art Gallery and Museum
Bridgeman Art Library, London

Printed in the United States of America

The paper used in this publication meets the minimum
requirements of the American National Standard for
Permanence of Paper for Printed Library Materials
Z39.48-1984.

Contents

Introduction, 1

Part 1. The Astrology of Sexuality
Understanding Sexuality, 4
The Sex Function, 10
Sex Karma, 24

Part 2. The Houses: Experiences through Polarity
The Houses, 28
The First and Seventh Houses, 30
The Second and Eighth Houses, 46
The Third and Ninth Houses, 67
The Fourth and Tenth Houses, 86
The Fifth and Eleventh Houses, 108
The Sixth and Twelfth Houses, 129

Part 3. Horoscopes
Sample Horoscope Delineations, 152
Allegory, 161

...To a richer understanding of one of our greatest inconstancies—our sexuality...

...To the very real people who are brave enough to admit that they are themselves...

...To the suffering, the agony, the sorrow, the pain, the joy, the learning, the unfoldment, and the evolution that we can only reach through sexuality— the core of our ability to feel!

Contents

Introduction, 1

Part 1. The Astrology of Sexuality
Understanding Sexuality, 4
The Sex Function, 10
Sex Karma, 24

Part 2. The Houses: Experiences through Polarity
The Houses, 28
The First and Seventh Houses, 30
The Second and Eighth Houses, 46
The Third and Ninth Houses, 67
The Fourth and Tenth Houses, 86
The Fifth and Eleventh Houses, 108
The Sixth and Twelfth Houses, 129

Part 3. Horoscopes
Sample Horoscope Delineations, 152
Allegory, 161

. . . To a richer understanding of one of our greatest inconstancies—our sexuality. . .

. . . To the very real people who are brave enough to admit that they are themselves. . .

. . . To the suffering, the agony, the sorrow, the pain, the joy, the learning, the unfoldment, and the evolution that we can only reach through sexuality— the core of our ability to feel!

Introduction

The perennial "battle of the sexes" has always been one of the most mystifying facts of life. Whether we are male or female, we want to be able to express and gain fulfillment from the sexual side of life. In order to find this fulfillment, we each must be able to understand sexuality and our role in it. There is a purpose to sex. There are reasons for it. There are lessons in it, and growth and evolvement comes from it. It is less important that we put value judgements on our sexuality than to understand the learning and growing process involved in it.

People marry for sexual reasons in our culture. They divorce for sexual reasons too. They have children as a result of sex. They buy products because of sex appeal. They dress to increase sexual attractiveness. They read books, go to movies, and expose themselves to different forms of mass media that have sexual nuances, overtones and flagrant instructions on how one can become a more sexual being. They confuse love with sex and sex with love. The largest business in the world is the cosmetic industry. The oldest business in the world is prostitution. How much of our everyday life is an interwoven tapestry of sexual thought and action? Consider your actions, thoughts and feelings in a single day and you will understand how little of life is not sexual. Even the individual who denies his or her sexuality is spending a great deal of energy denying it.

In supermarkets, many products are displayed with red labels — the color of the sex ray. It stimulates the astral body (ruled by Mars) to initiate the activity for purchase. The advertising industry plays on our need for sex as much as possible. They know that just below the threshold of conscious awareness, nearly every man and every woman is secretly experiencing sexual thoughts *all the time.* Some psychologists believe that on an average there are approximately five to seven sexually-related thoughts every second, and this is not even under conditions of sexual action.

We can see then, in terms of attitudes, expression of ego power, definition of worth, ability to successfully role-play, and ultimately the ability to fulfill one of mankind's most basic needs, sexuality is one of the primary moving forces in the world. Mankind can never experience "peace on earth" without understanding his sexuality first. Sex in all its forms is the avenue that leads to true harmony and understanding, or causes the frustrations that create untruths, arguments and, yes, even wars!

For most people it represents the area of their most difficult lessons. Through sex, an individual has the opportunity to see himself and others on the most personal of levels. Truth becomes unavoidable, where it is easily avoidable in other areas. A great deal of enlightment can come through sex, when we each learn what it is all about.

Part 1

The Astrology of Sexuality

1. Understanding Sexuality

The ocean of life is very deep. Every drop in the ocean is a sample of its entirty. Sexuality is one area where we as individuals can experience the whole world through another person. As one experiences his own sexuality with different people, he sees the same world in different facets and colors. Information which cannot be expressed verbally is exchanged on deeply intuitive levels. Glimpses of the great mystery may slowly unravel. It becomes easy to see how something as simple as sex can be as complex as the entire universe while at the same time as simple as creation itself.

Sex is the highest form of love that one can experience on a physical level. It opens up different centers in one's being and makes one vulnerable to his fellow human beings. It forces one to confront the aloneness of reality, and yet gives the opportunity to feel connected to it at the same time. It creates some of the most difficult life problems to work through because it is the last thing an individual must master before becoming truly a spiritual being. Many books have been written about the value of living the impersonal existence, but no one is capable of doing this until they have developed a centered understanding of what sexuality is all about. The right path in life is not a question of whether a person abstains from sex or overindulges in it. Instead, it is a question of whether or not he understands himself through his own sexuality in terms of it being one of the most direct paths toward the great mystery in life.

Sex generates enthusiasm and also creates exchanges of energy levels. It gives an individual a great "in-touchness" with his inner being, because it shows him all that is false. In this sense, it is a corrector and balancer of the ego because it shows an individual how really human he is. It can also strengthen the weak ego by showing a person that in his "basest, crudest" expression of himself he is still needed, appreciated and loved by another. It can make an individual confront what he may believe to be an "evil" instinct within himself and then proceed to show him that this instinct is not evil at all.

Most individuals have many sexually-rooted complexes which seem contradictory to each other. These are the different facets of one's being. When in the presence of one person, one facet will predominate. When in the presence of another, a different facet will show itself. This is a process through which we learn about ourselves. Some of these facets are pleasing and fulfilling. Some are not. All of them, however, are part of the great ocean in which we are each a single drop.

Some say sex is "dirty." But it is not. Some say sex is "clean." But it is not. Some say sex is perverse, but it is not that either. It is a force, an energy, a part of the Divine Inspiration that we are here to experience. On a personal level it represents humankind's greatest lesson, yet it is very much a part of his reason for being. Through being personal on a sexual level, man comes into contact with his higher centers and slowly begins to discover the great beauty within himself; for he is part of a beautiful world.

Neither the celibate nor the lecher knows the richness of the sexual experience for sex is not an extreme of life. Instead, it is the mainstream of existence itself. *It is the core of one's essence.* Every feeling we have about other people comes from what we unconsciously perceive as their sexual essence.

People spend years reading books, meditating, attending esoteric lectures, or studying mysticism in order to try to center themselves. They still tend to overlook the most obvious facet that is right in front of them. The front of one's body and the way we present it to another is really the symbolic plan for one's future, along with the display of all we have achieved up to this point. Study this sentence a bit as you think about it on very intimate levels. Some people are possessive. Some are not. But no matter how spiritual or non-possessive an individual may pretend to be, he is very much possessive of his body.

It is his identification. He may say that this is not so because he read books telling him that it should not be so. But that is not really being honest with himself. Even the celibate experiences great difficulty because he is going against this natural force within himself.

The purpose of sex is different for different people and different for those same people at different times in their evolution. On one level sex helps some people to overcome inhibitions which are preventing them from being all they could be in other areas in their lives. On another level, sex puts some people in tune with the truth of their natural instincts. They may come to know themselves better. On still another level, sex can bring out man's humanity to man. It can emphasize the fact that even though each person is a unique individual, no one is truly different from anyone else. For example, the ruler of a great nation, the servant on the lowest rung of the success ladder, or the slave who does not even know that there is a ladder are all equal when they confront their own sexuality. It is only one's sexuality consciousness, which is based upon the ability to love and to understand, that determines the richness of sex that one can experience.

Traditionally, astrologers considered sex to be largely a product of Mars, Venus, Uranus, Pluto, and the function of the Eighth House. The truth is that sex (just like anything else) is all a question of "mind," and when any person's mind is focused on sex, it is not only these factors that come into play. The entire horoscope symbolizes sexuality. All of the planets have an effect on a person's sex life. Could one communicate or even be conscious of a sexual thought without Mercury? Could one visualize a sexual image in the imagination without Neptune? If we limit our understanding of sexual astrology to a few planets, we would oversimplify what really takes place. The aspects, too, play a powerful role in how a person will behave sexually. Many squares in a chart may create strong sexual tensions while too many trines may show lethargy or disinterest. The signs that planets fall in are also important. An individual may have a planet receiving few aspects (or very weak ones) but this planet may be placed in a strongly-sexed sign which may activate the sexual energy. An unaspected Venus in Aries can be much stronger than Mars in Libra receiving many aspects.

We see, then, that the planets, the signs they fall in, and the aspects they receive all play different parts in the total picture of an individual's sexual makeup. What role do the houses play? We may find that the traditional method of interpreting sex through the eighth house is archaic. Does the fifth house (of love and romance) enter the picture? Can we ignore the fourth house (of emotional foundations)? What does the second house (of values) have to tell us? Astrologers should begin to realize that all the houses play their unique but integrated parts in the development of sexuality.

To understand the planets, signs, aspects, and houses all at once in terms of sexuality is naturally an unreasonable task. The question is then about where to begin. One fascinating characteristic of sexuality is that most people tend to experience it first and learn about it later! Children experiment with sexuality years before they are taught the so-called "facts of life." Adults learn the meaning of their own sexuality through the process of experimental experiences. Sex is a matter of experience. No one in the world can tell another person what sex is like if he has no experience. Extrapolating from this, it is most logical to begin our study of sexuality through that part of astrology which represents the world of experience. Of the four factors which have a role to play it is the astrological houses that represent the sexual incidents and events that occur in peoples lives, so we will look there first.

One of the most interesting facets of sexuality is how personally unique each individual tends to feel about himself. Few people believe that their own private sexual thoughts and feelings are shared by others. This causes alienation or a separation in a world that is trying to achieve oneness. One out of approximately fifteen people (because of intercepted houses) shares the same ideas, beliefs and experiences in their sexual lives. People are not really as different from each other as they try to believe. We can see this by understanding that each specific rising sign automatically sets up a basic polarity for the chart. A person with Cancer rising must have Capricorn on the seventh house. He probably has Leo on the second house, Aquarius on the eighth, Gemini on the twelfth and Sagittarius on the fifth. If no signs are intercepted, it's possible to know the polarity of the entire chart just from knowing the ascendant. Even when we don't know the chart from the ascendant, we know the seventh house, part of the sixth and eighth, and by polarity, part of the second and twelfth, as well.

A chart with Taurus rising will automatically have a Scorpio seventh house. It is likely that the second house will have Gemini in it, the eighth house will have Sagittarius in it, the sixth house will have Libra in it and the twelfth house will have Aries in it. We could continue along with this method for all the possible ascendants, but the point is that each rising sign automatically sets up a different chart polarity. These differences are seen not only on the ascendant, but through all the other houses that move with it. There are basically only twelve different possible polarities. The Cancer rising chart has a very specific feel that is basically different from a chart with Leo rising. In both instances, it is not just the rising sign, but the manner in which the charts are polarized along different vectors that ultimately keys us in to what is happening. When we think of sexual experiences, we are basically concerned with twelve different realms of expected occurrence. Naturally, planetary placements, aspects, intercepted signs and other factors in the horoscope shade these qualities and create differences within the sameness. These shadings are important and they will be explained in future volumes. The initial confrontation of one's sexuality can only reach the truth level when an individual realizes that his patterns of experience are humanistically shared by thousands upon thousands of others.

When two signs appear in the same house, it is wise to study both. Usually the sign on the house cusp gives the most accurate interpretation. In some cases planets appear in the second sign or the second sign fills appreciably more of the house, creating a strong tendency for the second sign to be playing a significant role in the individual's life experiences. It is also important to realize that the sign on the house cusp may be more apparent at earlier ages and the second sign surfaces as an individual becomes more aware of his own fullness.

In those rare instances where three signs fill a house, the individual may experience a great deal of karma concerning the manner in which he or she copes with the events symbolized by that house. While all three signs are important, a situation may occur where two signs are positive and one is negative, or two signs are negative and one is a positive polarity. Positive signs try to seek expression while the negative polarity signs tend to hide behind the positive signs for protection. The sign holding the most degrees in the house is extremely important. If it is a negative polarity it might only express itself under those conditions where the individual feels safe.

As we read the houses for the purpose of sexual interpretation a careful study of house size, positive-negative qualities, and planets in

the houses will show where the emphasis should be placed. It helps to understand the sex function as it becomes energized through the different planets. Houses that are ruled by certain planetary energies can be understood not only in terms of the house experiences but also through the effect of that planet's role in the "sex function."

2. The Sex Function

Sexuality and Energy

There will be much said about the different forms of sexual expression as they manifest themselves in life. It is important to remember that above all else sex is an *energy*. Because this is so, the way in which an individual either distorts his sexual life or leads a healthy sexual existence depends entirely upon his or her ability to learn how to flow with the current of that sexual energy. A person who runs away from it or who blocks his flow of sexual energy may experience many problems in other areas of life. The creative drive or instinct is based upon the sexual flow. Extremely creative individuals know how to balance the sexual energy so they can get the most benefit from this divine force. Individuals who sublimate, repress, or overexpress sexual energy on a physical level tend to lose the creative power. They may never experience an in-tunement with the source of energy that provides one's being with all possibilities and the strength to fulfill them.

We are often capable of more than we think. Most individuals, however, tend to think in unproductive mind loops. We begin a thought only to follow it through a complete circle and end up disappointed when we realize we are at the beginning again. In an effort to restructure our thinking processes, we begin the same loop over again. Much of life can be wasted in this form of "mental masturbation." Understanding how to use sexual energy to translate our life from thought to constructive activity is one of the most closely guarded mystical secrets. When we discover it—the principle is unbelievably simple.

Sexual energy is like the current of a river. It flows endlessly and it winds, curves and moves. The secret of fulfillment is to *flow with the current, seeing where it takes you,* rather than putting mental predispositions on the nature of the river or your relation to it. By either fighting or denying the sexual current, we tend to short-circuit. We neutralize our creative power and tend to lead a stagnant lifestyle. Most people who complain that they are not making the progress they want may not be flowing with their sexual current. They may be ignoring this abundant reservoir of creative energy that God has given us. Because of this, they may lack the understanding needed in order to generate new activities, new beginnings, to develop new proficiencies, to achieve fulfilling ends. Those who know how to flow with the sexual current are rich in whatever the mind conceives.

Sex and Fantasy

The planet Neptune is extremely important sexually because it is symbolic of all sex fantasy. There are few people who don't have sexual fantasies. For many, these wispy daydreams are the only way of coming in contact with the subtle unconscious. When we experience a sexual fantasy we are learning how to surface the subtle part of the unconscious as well as how to guide and control it. Sexual fantasy is similar to watching a movie in your mind. The imagination creates pictures, scenes, vignettes and stories in related sequences. These are all part of the sexual river. The conscious putting together of all these factors into a definite fantasy is one of the expressions of the creative mind learning how to ride the river. If all the different sexual factors in the unconscious remain disconnected, it is like a river flowing in seemingly purposeless directions without a central current that defines its essence.

When the conscious mind forms a sexual fantasy from the Neptunian impressions it absorbs, it is creating its own movie. It's important to realize that the ability to do this is the same as the ability to take other factors in life and put them together in some meaningful order. Sexual fantasy is far from being something that should inspire guilt or be forbidden, for it is, at the very least, the *essence* of the creative process. People who are unable to create sexual fantasy are unable to construct the boat through which they must ride the river of life. Instead they feel the sexual current and have difficulty relating to it. They may fear that it will take them away from themselves, or it may take them in directions they are unaccustomed to or afraid of. The current itself is definitely a Plutonian force, but when we can combine illusion with energy, the Neptunian sexual illusion or fantasy acts as a buffer for the raw energy. We can deal with the unknown (Pluto) by creatively making it known (Neptune). The raw energy then becomes channeled through the imagination in creative fantasy.

Sex and Magnetism

Uranus is the planetary symbol of sexual magnetism. When someone has many sexual fantasies, he tends to attract many people. The combinatin of the fantasy (Neptune) with the magnetism (Uranus) creates a charismatic force in the personality structure. Consider the person who doesn't fantisize. In such a person there is no associative link between Uranus (magnetic qualities) and Pluto (the sexual current). While he may attract people through the Uranus placement, he is unable to imagine (Neptune) how to constructively use the current he feels. In such cases the combination of Uranus and Pluto may express in unpleasant ways rather than with the touch of divine love that is inherent in Neptune.

The magnetic quality of sex is never really a physical thing. People believe that they are attracted to each other because of physical characteristics but that may not be the case. Uranus represents a magnetic energy that vivifies, electrifies, and gives intensity to whatever exists on the subtle (Neptune) and gross (Pluto) unconscious layers. The most beautiful female or the most handsome male with a weak Uranus will have less sexual magnetism than those people who may be less attractive but who exhude a strong Uranian magnetic field in the aura. Sexual pictures and impressions may remain in the Neptune layers of the imagination unless they are sparked by Uranus.

The Sex Wall

Pluto symbolizes the raw sexual current, Neptune symbolizes the experience of creative fantasy which is further excited by Uranus. But what an individual does from this point on depends on how he relates to Saturn—the sex wall. Energy is one thing—imagination and fantasy are another. Sexual excitement is still another. None of these words describe sex activity. They are activities going on within the individual and are not yet manifested in the outside world.

When these activities are being pushed towards expression by Uranus, each of us confronts the Saturn wall before being able to express sex in reality. We cope with our personal standards, scruples, repressions, sublimations, parental or religious teachings, as well as the cautious pattern symbolized by Saturn. We fear rejection. It is at this point that we all wonder if we are capable of bringing the inner sex activities into form. This is an extremely interesting phenomenon of the sex experience because it helps explain what happens to us when we repress all that has built up through Pluto, Neptune, and Uranus. Instead of moving ahead through Saturn, the inner sex activity may be blocked by the same outer planets it comes from. In essence, it retrogrades back into the inner self, causing extreme frustration. Instead of symbolizing the possibility for a higher form of awareness, the outer planets remain filled with crude sex energy (Pluto), unrequited fantasies (Neptune), and nervous excitement (Uranus). If we use our Saturn to bind ourselves to the outer planets we can become incapable of understanding the higher levels of ourselves that can occur when the outer planet energy is freed.

The individual who moves through the Saturn wall, however, is able to tap into a clearer channel of this information which puts him in tune with the universe. Since information is always carried by energy, the more information available, the greater the sexual energy as well. The sex drive is replenished. The ability to move the inner sex activity through the wall of Saturn is part of a natural process that energizes both the sexual and the creative flow. Naturally, information, knowledge, and wisdom are part of this very same flow. The ability to break through the Saturn wall is an integral part of the growing process. The inability to break through the Saturn wall symbolizes a stagnation that may be the result of crystallizing old patterns that should be changing as we mature.

Sex Risk—Sex Freedom

If Saturn is used as a preparation for sexual expression rather than an inhibiting wall, then Jupiter can represent the last part of what one must work through. Jupiter symbolizes where we come out from behind the mask of Saturn and become vulnerable. All the inner sex activity is brought forward toward experience. In a sense, we all experience risk through Jupiter, because we come out of ourselves and make known our intention to experience sexual freedom. It is interesting to note that once an individual has been able to bring the inner sexual activity to Jupiter, many of the sexual fears, inhibitions, anxieties, and mind blocks quickly fall away. Jupiter's promise of reward for effort assures one of hope. Optimistic expansion tends to pervade and the risk factor diminishes.

Since Jupiter symbolizes the last part of the experience within oneself, it shows some interesting physical characteristics. It is the largest of the planets. It symbolizes a tendency to exaggerate, and if the smooth flow through Saturn has been effective it is a factor in heightening the enjoyment of the sexual experience. On the other hand, some people come to the sex activity with one foot in Jupiter and one foot in Saturn. They only come through the "wall" enough to partially experience Jupiter, and they keep themselves half behind the wall for the sake of security. One manifestation can be seen in the person who is confronted with a sexual situation he wants to experience but only talks about, using Jupiter's repetitive qualities as a device to dissapate the energy until the reason for fulfilling the sex act (Saturn and all the planets behind it) is too unfocused to continue. Most sex problems occur somewhere between the symbols Saturn and Jupiter. Healthy normal sexuality proceeds through Jupiter's expansive feeling of the inner sex activities to Mars (the first of the personal planets).

One can feel sexuality (Pluto), imagine it (Neptune), experience inner magnetic excitement (Uranus) and feel the need to put it in form (Saturn) by abandoining all impediments to the flow of current (Jupiter). But it is not until one takes the first step in initiating sex action (Mars) that sex becomes a personal and intimate endeavor. Here all the richness of the outer planets is focused into the personal part of one's being.

The Good—Evil Quality

Many individuals have experienced that sex carries with it tinges of the "good-evil" syndrome. On a spiritual level we say that it shouldn't—but it often does. There is reason for this. Originating from Pluto, from the very depths of the unconscious where mankind stores away unacceptable thoughts, the sex urges must move through Saturn, where our judgemental qualities act as a filter before it is freed through Jupiter. These two planets, Saturn and Jupiter act as the balancers between restriction and expression. They symbolically weigh each sexual situation carefully and give each person the opportunity to understand his personal role before he acts. The outer planets represent the rules of the culture and the time in history just prior to our personalizing the role we will play in the sex act.

In truth, sex is neither good nor evil. It just is. When an individual is attempting to bring the inner sex-activity into personal focus there is much yin and yang in terms of social acceptance (as represented by the sexual partner). Each person wants to feel there is sanction in doing whatever he or she needs. At this point, the ego of the partner becomes the focus of social acceptance.

Outer Sexual Expression

There is a big difference between inner sex activity and outer sex activity. One involves the creative process stemming from the self, while the other meets the self-mirror through a partner. Once sex activity moves outward, it enters the law of cause and effect in the outer world. Action and reaction become interwoven. In the inner sex activity there is still cause and effect (action and reaction) but both roles are being played by different parts of the same person. In the outer activity this is no longer so.

Mars rules the astral or desire body. As we begin to experience outer sex activity, we start to project the mirror of inner thoughts onto a partner. As a result of these projections (causes) there are reactions from the partner (effects). It is important to realize that all outer sexual expression depends upon the partner receiving and acting out the projected mirror. At the same time, the partner has a mirror of his own.

Are we saying that during sexual expression, individuals are really having sex with themselves? Yes, but the difference between the inner sex activity and the outer expression is that in the outer expression each individual is really helping the other to have sex with himself. While this exists, it is not true on all levels, nor is it true for all people. Since individuals differ, one's astral mirror may easily dominate another. When this occurs we think of the person as being sexually selfish. The aggressive nature of Mars must be experienced in order to filter the inner sex activity through the personal ego. Some people have to do it in "selfish" ways while others have a much more expansive ego and do not need a strong astral mirror. The point is that this is a stage at which the free thoughts symbolized by Jupiter become focused through the personal quality of Mars to bring about physical sex. Whether the male or the female takes the leading role will depend upon two factors. First, the indiviudal who is looking at himself most will invariably dominate the experience. Second, we must understand that some individuals are able to experience sex all the way through this point without ever coming completely through the wall of Saturn. People who complain that they are unable to reach orgasm are unable to let go of their Saturnian defenses. They are not fully present in the act itself. Since Saturan is the planet of Karma, these individuals are working through sex karma with every act. The more they learn how to use Jupiter and Mars, the easier it is for them to move through Saturn. Slowly they learn their karmic lessons.

The Love Experience

As Mars energy is expended, sex changes to incorporate feelings of love and the activity moves to Venus. The harsh impatience of the Mars phase changes to gentle caring and tenderness as the energy is transmuted into a more gentle energy. The need for expression develops a need for giving and sharing. The friction of Mars becomes a delicate blending of energies as an exchange of energies is experienced. The male absorbs the female energy at this stage. The female absorbs the male energy. It is at this point where the male feels more feminine. The female feels more masculine. Through the absorption of male energy she is able to experience the yang of quality of life. As the male absorbs her energy he experiences the yin quality. Thus, the love experience adds balance to what would otherwise be incomplete sexual expression. Some individuals have difficulty reaching this stage. They avoid the absorption of opposite sex energy which stops the flow of the sexual experience at Mars. By trying to hold onto the ego, sex becomes separated from love and they miss the very important energy exchange that takes place through Venus.

Understanding

One of the biggest problems between people has always been communication. People are just not able to talk about what they mean to each other. Instead they circumvent, avoid, use illogical thought patterns and whatever other devices they can invent to keep themselves from conveying the ideas they so badly need to convey. Once a man has the female energy in him, he can understand her. In essence, he is her. The two have become one in mind. At the same time, her absorption of his energy enables her to understand him, for she is him as well as herself. This is the function of Mercury. Crude sex energy is too powerful to be handled by the mental centers in the body, but once it has been expressed through Mars and softened through Venus, it slowly rises to these same mental centers. The result is a mutual understanding between individuals which could not occur through any process other than sex. All of the understanding that each individual has as a gift for the other (stored in the outer planets) has been filtered, refined and gently transferred as the love experience is accepted by both partners. The understanding that comes from this transfer is experienced by those who realize after sex that they seem to be on the other person's wavelength for quite a while. There is a meshing of frequencies between the partners. If the sex activity goes all the way to Mercury, this blending into a singular frequency is extremely fulfilling and may last for weeks. Sex that ends before the harmonious transfer of energies through Venus is much less fulfilling, establishes a weaker link between the two and needs to be repeated more often with less benefit.

We have seen how sexual activity begins as crude energy (Pluto) that moves from the outermost planet inward, until it finally reaches overt expression starting with Mars. It continues inward on intimate personal levels, ultimately (when it can) reaching Mercury which symbolizes that very special form of communication that sex truly is.

Fulfillment

The ability to release pent-up emotions is possible only when an individual knows that his most private thoughts can be understood and accepted. The Moon symbolizes the reflection of the self in an attempt to find acceptance and can only be fulfilled after sexual activity has reached the level of understanding through Mercury. This complete fulfillment may also be a part of the symbolic returning to the womb. The indivudual feels that he or she has been nourished totally by the correct understanding source. Thus, emotional orgasm is possible. Many people experience a physical orgasm, but few know what an emotional orgasm is about. They believe that because their bodies are tired, drained or no longer able to continue the sex act, or because they have secreted certain hormones that they have indeed reached orgasm. This is only on a physical level. The mental orgasm occurs through Mercury when we realize that we are fully understood by another. The emotional orgasm occurs through the Moon, when the home within oneself if reached. The Moon nourishes, and through its ability to retain memories, it can carry the strength of a single creative sexual experience within us for quite some time. It gives a feeling of birth, along with the emphasis to move forward in other areas of life.

One

When this complete orgasm is achieved, we have used all of our planets except the Sun, the basic idealistic perfect self. The birth feeling that results from the emotional orgasm of the Moon brings us to the center of being from which all else will emanate. We find that the sexual activities start from an unresolved state (ten planets) and end with the blossoming of our center through our Sun. It is like a funneling of energies toward that one focal point of being that we always strive to attain.

Aspects and Sex Activity

The different aspects between the planets gives us important clues as to how the sex activity is functioning in any one horoscope. A harmonious aspect between any planet and the next innermost planet makes it relatively easy for the sex function to progress. A difficult aspect between any planet and the next innermost planet usually symbolizes a stopping point in the sex process where the individual must learn how to overcome difficulties. For example, a trine or conjunction between Pluto and Neptune indicates it is easy for the individual to add creative fantasy to the raw sexual energy. Another harmonious aspect between Neptune and Uranus indicates it is easy for the individual to become aroused by his or her fantasies. If the horoscope shows a square between Uranus and Saturn, however, the sexual activity often becomes blocked at "the sex wall," and needs help in overcoming obstacles if it is to proceed. Using this method, we can see from chart to chart the manner in which the sex function proceeds smoothly and how it presents problems for an individual. Consider the horoscope of Sigmund Freud, who spent much of his life attempting to understand the sexual function.

The only aspects drawn in on the chart are those which progress from outer planets inward, thus showing the flow of the sexual function.

There is no aspect between Pluto and Neptune indicating that Freud would not have experienced an easy flow between the crude sexual energy to the fantasy layers of the imagination. In fact, he spent much of his life trying to understand this. Ultimately he published a book entitled, *The Interpretation of Dreams*. He advanced the theory that the symbols in dreams were meaningful because of what they represented from the crude unconscious (Pluto), but he never really understood this function in the creative process himself. The sextile from Neptune to Uranus indicated that he was in touch with how dreams and fantasies lead to excitation, but the absence of an aspect between Urnaus and Saturn shows still another area where Freud put in much effort in order to reach some

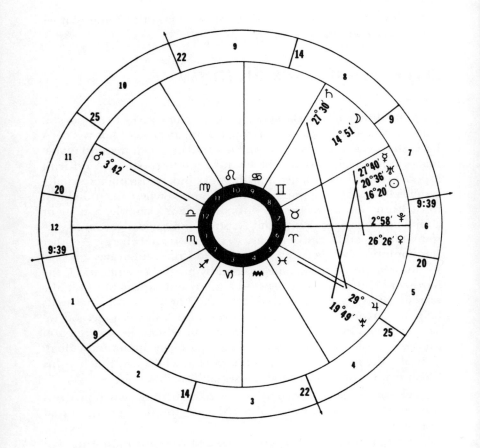

Sigmund Freud
May 6, 1856
Freiburg, Czechoslovakia

Birth data obtained from *An Astrological Who's Who* by Marc Penfield, Arcane Publications, York Harbor, Maine, 1972, p. 169.

understanding. Through the Neptune-Uranus aspect, he could intuitively sense the magnetic sexual qualities that lay dormant behind Saturn's walls, but much of his work was in probing into the repressions, guilt syndromes, sublimations, and other impediments to sex expression that he found in his own Saturn.

There is an aspect between Saturn and Jupiter, but it is a square, indicating the tensions he experienced between the traditional cultural mores which inhibitied sex expression and the honesty of Jupiter's desire for release from bondage. The opposition between Jupiter and Mars shows conflict between the last phase of inner sex activity and the first phase of outer sex expression. Here Freud advanced the concept of the superego as a means of explaining why people internalize their environment and have difficulties in their outer sex expression because of it. Perhaps the most interesting thing in the entire chart is the lack of an aspect between Mars and Venus (traditionally called the two sexual planets). In spite of the intensity of his work, he never really explored the concept of the energy which occurs during the love experience in the Venus phase. This is important because it shows us something about how to read sex activity from a chart. Whenever an aspect is missing between any planet and the next inner planet, the sex activity is momentarily thwarted. It is seeking the next sequential planet but must divert itself through other aspects in order to reach it. In Freud's chart, Mars must move back through Saturn (expressing the square aspect) before it can reach Venus indirectly (Saturn sextile Venus). From Freud's point of view sex could not be seen as leading directly to the love experience. He felt its overt expression (leading back to Saturn) would often reveal hidden complexes, blocks, impediments to natural healthy feelings, and a host of other restrictions that stand in the way of someone's ability to feel love. It is because of his aspects that Freud was never really able to put the puzzle together although he made great starts in understanding sexuality.

He did not know that love brings understanding. We see this through his Venus-Mercury semi-sextile aspect. Because of his Mars to Saturn to Venus direction, he would have great difficulty realizing the continuous flow of sex energy in the way that it is meant to work. His realization of love as the foundation for understanding would have been much more on a hypothetical basis than founded upon any personal awareness of the potential of the sexual flow.

Sexual Relationships

All people have a different blend of energies that are emitted from their auras. Some people are strongly Neptunian types. There is a vague gossamer quality about them that can give an impression that is soothing to others. Some people are very Uranian. They bubble with excitement and exhileration and always bring a charge to the atmosphere of their environment. Most of the time one planet or another strongly defines our particular vibration. This factor plays an important role in sexual relationships.

For sexual fulfillment to be complete, the sex activity must be able to proceed as smoothly as possible from Pluto all the way to Mercury. If one does not have the necessary Neptune aspects he tends to be strongly attracted to Neptunian types who emanate enough of the Neptune vibration to fill the gap. In this same way, any planet lacking aspects (or having difficult aspects) tends to attract individuals whose chart fills these missing links.

This is the reason why we relate intensely to some people and less intensely with others. The individuals through whom we complete ourselves become important to us. Through them we come to understand how the smooth flow of sex activity is supposed to work.

Since Pluto has a great deal to do with mass consciousness, and what an individual unconsciously absorbs from his environment, this same progression to Mercury is also important in terms of how the learning process works. In horoscopes having harmonious aspects from Pluto all the way to Mercury, learning is a smooth-flowing experience. Where there are difficult or missing aspects, the ability to learn becomes impeded. In the same manner as sexual fulfillment, we need other people to explain ideas, thoughts, and concepts that fill the gaps or spaces shown in our chart. Learning and sex are not isolated experiences, nor are they necessarily separate from each other. Many people experience their greatest learning through sex. Even when sex is not expressed in physical form, its undercurrent of energy moving through the planets becomes a basis for the continuity of learning. Thoughts that are taken from Pluto to Mercury are easily understood because they have gone through the colors of all the different planetary energies in between. Thoughts or concepts that stop somewhere in the middle of the process are felt to be incomplete; they may lack depth and clarity.

Sexual relationships are rarely for sex alone. They exist so that individuals can learn. It is the sexual experience which opens the door for our learning channels. Through this path, we come to understand the importance of continuity. In constructive relationships, the mind gains focus through its ability to follow the current. It trains itself to accept nothing less than what it can be. The misfortune of unhappy experiences lies in the scattering of our learning energies. If the mind becomes accustomed to indirect currents, it ceases to function at its most optimum levels.

We can see that all relationships influence how the mind learns to direct thought. Since all experience arises in the mind first, the proper channeling of all that the mind perceives is an important quality to develop. We find that different sexual experiences leave imprints in the mind. By opening certain channels and memory centers, they become roadmaps of future thought. If sex and learning are linked in this fashion it is easy to understand why sex plays such an important role in the evolution of mankind.

3. Sex Karma

A great deal of Karma (the law of cause and effect*) occurs as the result of sexual experiences. Different parts of the physical body remember each experience as well as bringing many unconscious memories of the past into new experiences. The accumulated effects of varied sexual experiences in past lives act as the cause of how an individual may relate to sex in the present life. While on the surface this seems merely academic, its implications are quite deep psychologically.

Many people may unconsciously confuse present sexual actions with hidden memories of past experiences. As long as this occurs sexual lessons will be learned in terms of how one truly and honestly is capable of relating to another.

There are many levels of sex; they range from the most crude experiences that contain only lust or alienation to the highest forms that symbolize the pure essence of divine love through human expression. Through different lifetimes or different experiences in this lifetime, people can gradually learn how to reach sexual fulfillment as they slowly filter out mere magnetic attraction to sex and make room for the higher forms of sexual love.

On the lower levels of sex karma, there may be a retention of past beliefs that form the identity structure. The sex act may represent very

---

*See Martin Schulman, *Karmic Astrology, Vols. 1-4,* (York Beach, ME: Samuel Weiser).

little sharing or caring for the inner needs of the other person. Sex may appear to be separated from love. If someone does not understand that sex is not a battle or a contest for the ego, the euphoric qualities of love that are present on the higher levels are usually absent.

On a somewhat higher level of sexual consciousness an awareness that the sex act can produce certain feelings both in the self and the partner and have a lasting effect on the future of the relationship begins to manifest. This is where people begin to be cognizant of karmic implications. Sex is a form of communication. Often it is the door-opener between people who would otherwise seem isolated from each other. A bond is created that will forever influence how each one will feel about the other.

On truly high levels of sexual experience an awareness of the presence of cosmic love appears. The lower self is transcended. People, places, time and space all become part of the one universal mind that rules all. On this level, a *blending* of two individuals takes place.

The goal of sex is not only physical gratification. Nor is it only emotional fulfillment. It isn't even the achievement of mental understanding. It is the unification of two souls melting into the cosmic oneness that is their divine legacy.

Sex is a multi-faceted experience and the love expressed in physical form serves not only the function of learning how to intimately relate to another, but to impersonally recreate God's symbolic act of creation.

Sex karma implies many intricate threads much like those interwoven in a tapestry that slowly moves towards completion. Whatever our sexual level is we will automatically attract two distinct types of people to us. One type represents our sexual teachers while the other symbolizes our sexual students. Each of us can see where we have been and where we are going at any given time. We are often most comfortable with people whose sexual evolvement is from our past, and we stay in our past as long as we vibrate on that level. We may not be comfortable with those whose sexual evolvement symbolizes all we are evolving toward. If we are willing to learn something "higher" we will unquestionably make much karmic progress—not only in the sexual area, but also in coming closer to a fuller understanding of our being and our place in the world.

Sex opens up sensitivity centers in the body. It is for this reason that conversations held just after sexual experiences are extremely deep, often reaching right to the core of the unconscious. This is a positive experience because many profound realizations are reached this way. However, a steady diet of too much sex may cause too much sensitivity to the outside world. The amount of sexual experience we engage in at any given time should be proportionate to what we can assimilate in terms of awarenesses that help our growth. And sex without awareness is basically wasteful and karmically stagnant.

It is important that each of us work on evolving our sexual level, because by doing this we are helping to create a more humane culture to live in. As individuals learn how to be more fulfilled, so does the world as a whole.

We often think of sex karma in relation to how an individual acts. There is sex karma in non-action also. Sexual energy is a very fine energy that moves rapidly through the body. Mental energy is a more coarse energy and slower movement allows one to think clearly. When a person has a physiological need to release sex energy and inhibits it for any psychological reason, the sex energy may overflow into the mental centers. This causes irritation, muddled thinking, anger, distorted concepts, and a great deal of irrational reasoning. It is important for a person to know his sexual needs so he is able to maintain a balance between sexual energies and other life energies.

When a slight amount of sexual energy spills over to the mental centers, it produces eagerness, stimulates the thought processes, and gives a person the incentive to do things he may not have thought himself capable of. When practically no sexual energy moves through the body, a general feeling of lethargy pervades one's being, and the result may be laziness or depression. Individuals who are sexually-balanced are a pleasure to be with for they are generally happy, appear to have both feet on the ground, and are capable of contributing to society. People who don't balance sexual energy walk around with guilt, fear, tension, body aches; they are basically a drain on relatives, friends and society.

The direction of a person's life is determined by the sexual energy level he vibrates, and the way in which it is being handled. We eventually learn that sex, rather than being a baser part of life is really the most natual part of existence; and the balance that can integrate the lower with the higher self.

Part 2

The Houses: Experiences through Polarity

4. The Houses

The twelve astrological houses represent systematic experiences. These experiences progress from the first through the twelfth house in sequential order. In the first house an individual learns about his identity. Once he or she has done this, it becomes possible to discover the meaningful value systems symbolized by the second house. These values can be communicated to others through the third house. As this system continues throughout the zodiacal wheel, an individual begins to understand a complete life experience.

Although these experiences are different they are not unrelated. The events, circumstances, and behavior patterns of each house, rather than being interpreted on an isolated basis, can be seen with greater clarity through the interplay of the houses which are polar opposites. In the same way that each zodiac sign bears a strong relationship to its opposite sign, the houses follow analogously. Differences between Aries and Libra, for example, are similar to differences between the first and seventh houses. Differences between Taurus and Scorpio are similar to differences between the second and eighth house, and so on throughout the wheel.

These differences are not as much differences as they are opposing sides of the same coin. The first and seventh house symbolize the polarity of a particular type of coin inasmuch as they represent a certain kind of experience. The second and eighth house represent a different kind of experience; or a different type of coin. Opposites are too often viewed as opposites without the realization that a dichotomy can only exist when there is a central truth binding both sides of that something together. The two sides of a coin may appear to be different, but in fact they are very much part of the same thing. Two sides of any disagreement cannot exist without the central issue of the disagreement which is common to both. When we study the effects of astrological houses, we must realize that although we see a yin-yang polarity in opposite houses, the polarity also represents something which is common to both.

As an individual grows through learning about himself, it is never the uncentered view of any extreme that resolves problems or difficulties, but rather understanding the central essence of all extremes.

5. The First and Seventh Houses

The first and seventh house symbolize the experiences needed for the devolpment and identification of Self—in relation to its essential essence as well as its reflection through others.

In the first house the expression of the ego takes place as the individual establishes his sense of self-worth. Here we try to see our uniqueness in the world of sexual competition. As the house of physical appearance, the first house symbolizes the subjective view of one's sexual attractiveness.

The first thoughts of sex are usually tied in with ego-indentification. In this Mars-ruled house the energy of the libido seeks to build an individual's ego strength through personal expression. Since the first house is the focal lens that filters the rest of the chart if a person is to reach fulfillment, it is quite natural for this part of the horoscope to symbolize self-aggrandizement. If an individual does not do this for himself he holds the remainder of the chart inside himself.

A balance can be achieved through the function of the seventh house. The subjective views of the first house can be objectively mirrored as the individual sees himself in the eyes of a spouse or those with whom he is intimately connected. One's identity structure is basically made up of the perception of subjective reality (first house) and the understanding of objective reality (seventh house). The thoughts and feelings one has of oneself often needs external confirmation so that belief in one's identity can be soundly established.

Most people are capable of seeing others more clearly than they can see themselves. This happens because the ego (as symbolized by the first house) is the closest understanding of himself that an individual has. The ego-ideal (as symbolized by the seventh house) contains within it all that we would like to be if we could reach our ideal self image. There is a natural tendency for the ego of the first house (ruled by Mars) to aggressively reach for the ego-ideal of the seventh (ruled by Venus).

When the ego appears to be far below the ego-ideal, the person senses a general state of incompleteness. Through marriage or close relationships with others he may be able to find the qualities that fill this gap and gradually add them to his image of self through a process of osmosis. As this occurs, the ego and the ego-ideal grow closer together, and a general state of contentment and happiness ensues. This is the natural balance of the first and seventh house. Together they complete two sides of the same coin.

We do not live in an isolated reality. All that we develop through our ego demands feedback from others so we can know if we are putting our life on a correct course. The first and seventh houses act like mirrors of each other. Marriage (as symbolized by the seventh house) can be a unifying experience which thrives on the contributory efforts of individualistic endeavor (as symbolized by the first house).

Aries First House— Libra Seventh House

With Aries in the first house, the individual is developing a new identity structure in this incarnation. His drive may appear primitive to others. There may be sexual anxiety due to the feeling that so much lies ahead that needs to be accomplished and this person doesn't have the practice or resources with which to do it.

This individual needs spontaneous fulfillment in order to build the faith in himself that will ultimately give him feelings of self-worth. It is not the sex act itself that he subconsciously needs as much as what it represents—a challenge that he is capable of conquering.

This gives him the strength to carry his pioneering spirit into other areas of life.

The more he is able to make new beginnings, the better he can fulfill a deep need within himself to prove that he is not inferior. Basically shy underneath (from the hidden twelfth house, Pisces), his anxiety actually creates situations that would not otherwise exist. By doing this, he gives himself a chance to overcome the inadequacies he feels.

With Aries in the first house, sexual sublimation causes headaches and other stress related difficulties and diseases. The individual not only needs a partner who encourages sexual expression, but also one who will let him win the symbolic contest. However, if he wins all the time, he can lose interest in the partner. On the surface, it may appear that he is trying to prove his superiority, but unconsciously he wants to be noticed and appreciated by his mate.

The Libra seventh house can act as a mirror for desires that arise as a consequence of having an ego. When he looks at this mirror of himself, he may realize that his dream is not to strive to outdo everybody, nor to feel constantly driven toward success, but rather to experience the peace of mind that a harmonious relationship can bring. A close union with another can teach him how to balance the Libra characteristics of non-desire with the compulsive strivings of his ego. His mate is usually altrustic and adaptible, and can show him the counterpoint of his excessive narcissistic obsessions with his personal self.

The inherent lesson in this house polarity is the differences and blendings between sex and love. The ego seeks sexual conquest (Aries in the first house) but the ego-ideal is more interested in a lighter, more ethereal love experience (Libra in the seventh). The ultimate balance is the understanding that love and sex are not isolated from each other. Instead, sex adds richness and depth to the love experience, while love adds beauty, rhyme and reason to sex.

KEYWORDS: competitive ego, cooperative partner, inspiration from mate, spontaneous sex drive, affectionate marriage, strong libido, primitive instinct, sharp, aggressive, adventurous, learns cooperation through marriage, self-conscious, sensitive to relationships, sometimes bi-sexual feelings, seeks fairness from others, gains balance through marriage.

Taurus First House—
Scorpio Seventh House

The Taurus first house represents an extremely loving personal nature. The Scorpio seventh house often attracts highly-sexed partners who fulfill unconscious insecurities in the ego.

There is strong sexual interest in a variety of partners, yet this individual has a basic tendency to cling to one person. Being keenly attuned to physical sensations, his sense of touch and smell are probably the highest developed in the entire zodiac. Physical love is essential to the ego while raw lust creates the transformation that surfaces the ideals of the higher self. It may be difficult for this individual to accept friendships with the opposite sex on a purely platonic level. As a young adult, when these situations are presented to him, he may experience strong inner feelings of rejection which are difficult to recognize. To compensate for this, he may be excessive in all his endeavors usually wanting the opposite sex to recognize his physical strength and endurance. Both sexes may have difficulty being completely loyal to one partner.

The earthy qualities of sex are seen as primary needs and he may have difficulty keeping a perspective. This house polarity functions on raw instinct which creates a feeling of "realness" in the identity structure. With Scorpio in the seventh, there may be some disparity between the basic qualities of the ego and the hectic lifestyle it experiences through intimate involvements with others. Transformations occur through divorce or broken relationships as the ego-ideal is striving for some unknown quality that is deeper and more mystical than what is at hand. There is a tendency to be bored with the self, while intrigued with others. As a result, this person attracts individuals who are keenly perceptive, highly intuitive, and often psychic. They may see him better than he sees himself. He often depends on their vision and insight in order to understand the deeper motivations of his actions.

With this placement, relationships are extremely intense, often highly romantic, volatile, and non-permanent. These relationships are necessary to transform an ego that is otherwise highly resistant to change.

The lesson in this house polarity is to learn how to help others transform their values while still retaining self-identity.

KEYWORDS: sensuous, sexual relationships, basic, earthy, crude or lustful partner, possessive tendencies, jealous of self, indulgent, develops depth through marriage, experiences volatile sexual transformations. paranoid feelings, divorce likely, strong survival instinct.

Gemini First House— Sagittarius Seventh House

This individual seeks to understand the higher truths in relationships. Through sex, he can act out both his own role and that of his partner so that he can understand both sides of the experience. With all his desire for fairness, understanding and liberation of thought, he may discover that his sex partners are more free than he is. He may seek people younger than himself and through these spontaneous relationships he develops the sparkling presence that the Gemini ascendant exhudes. A great deal of mental activity often leads to a variety of short sexual experiences rather than deeply-committed sexual involvements. It is not sexual competition that is the goal here. Instead, it is the ability to take a non-sexual situation into a sexual reality. This individual learns how to integrate love's dreams with their expression in the real world.

With Sagittarius in the seventh, the ego-ideal is based on truth and honesty. Above all else, the individual values these factors as something so extra special that no quality can rise above them. These ideals balance the dual nature of the ego. Gemini symbolizes the twin minds. There is always a "yes-no" quality to the identity structure. This yin and yang tends to create child-like insecurities within one's basic perception of self, which disappears in relationships that bring out the higher mind qualities of Sagittarius for Sagittarius can see the dualities and yet know the oneness of truth that is above all doubt. With this house polarity, the individual can only feel centered through the objective light that comes from relating to another. As a result there is a tendencey to practically idolize a mate who is able to view things from a philosophically-detached vantage point.

The ego views sex as a curious play in which it is both the actor and the observer. At the same time, the individual attracts partners who bring out the ideals of the higher self in terms of honesty, sincerity, and the sense of freeing one's spirit from the mundane. Ironically, the individual with a Sagittarius seventh house feels most free when he knows he belongs to somebody.

The lesson of this house polarity is to free the self through marriage by understanding the way in which the dual nature of the ego communicates with its ideals.

KEYWORDS: mentally agressive, spontaneous, youthful, dual identity structure, repetitive sexual patterns, versatile, adaptible, talkative during sex, exhibitionist tendencies, fortune through marraige, eclectic.

Cancer First House—
Capricorn Seventh House

Here sexuality is strongly linked to emotional security. This individual is highly sensitive and keenly intuitive. He may be attracted to older people so he can learn how to mature on a sexual level. Unable to deal with rejection, he may avoid making any advances toward the opposite sex if he feels the slightest possibility of rejection. Love is not taken lightly. Being intimate with someone means a committment on many levels, and as a result, this individual becomes strongly attached to anyone who sincerely shows him affection.

A childlike shyness makes this individual seek a strong partner for protection. In addition, sexual response is linked to trust. When he feels this trust, he's extremely warm and loving and can be an able giver without questioning how much. Although the ego is strongly rooted in emotionality, the ego-ideal needs to achieve maturity. As a result, this individual will seek a mate who can pull out his potential in every way possible.

Through his ego (first house), he often becomes enthusiastic about feelings that strike spontaneously, and needs the mirror of Capricorn to determine if these feelings are practical or simply a childish display of emotions. On a sexual level, some Oedipal conflict may need to be worked out. Marriage may be a re-enactment of childhood roles in order that past emotional residue can be organized into some form of logic upon which security can be built.

Basically frightened of the outside world, he has a need for constant reassurance. This may cause a dependency which puts this person at the mercy of his partner, who always seems to manage to bring situations under control. Or he may resent the fact that he needs a partner to take care of him.

To build emotional security, he may marry an older mate or someone whose sense of honor, dignity and self-respect is above reproach. The ego is like a budding flower reaching for the ideal of the esteem it desires when it forms into a mature bloom.

This house placement symbolizes one of the most important sexual lessons in the zodiac. If one is to ever taste the essence of fulfillment, then one must understand that sexual love is based on vulnerability. The Cancer ascendant needs to be vulnerable in order to express the full gamut of emotions it feels, but it can only open up when the individual intuitively knows that security accompanies the sexual act.

KEYWORDS: emotional, sensitive, warm, impulsive, childlike, sensuous, possessive, hides feelings, forms strong attachments, embarrasses easily, very fertile, maternal instinct, karmic marriage to older partner, values protectiveness, enduring relationships, private personage, grows through marriage.

Leo First House—
Aquarius Seventh House

With this placement there may be exhibitionism in many areas. This person is symbolic of the full flower in its bloom reaching for the Sun. There is a strong ego and a sound self-image. Although this person is highly-sexed, he will nevertheless avoid situations which would demean his personal sense of self-esteem.

Hidden love affairs become the proving grounds through which he expresses his natural creative and romantic instincts. Because there is an air of royalty associated with the identity structure, he may feel the sexual experiences he desires should not be denied to him. In many ways he may put himself above the domination of others. He seeks attention and is attracted to anyone who has the slightest tinge of voyeurism.

The Aquarius seventh house acts as a balance to the powerful ego drives that never quite seem to be fulfilling. The impersonal need to be of service to humanity acts through marriage as a means of focusing the veritable powerhouse of the Leo ascendant. Although the individual needs marriage to achieve his goal, there is some difficulty in maintaining an enduring relationship with one mate. The entire concept of an intimate relationship violates the ego-ideals of Aquarius which are impersonal and detached in intimate situations.

Divorce is common with this placement, but can be avoided if the mate is non-demanding and philosophically able to understand the idea of mutual independence within the state of marriage. On a sexual level, there is never a blending of two egos into one, as both Leo and Aquarius have very powerful wills. Instead each individual is teaching the other how to be "their own person." The closeness and warmth that one might expect in a marriage is not truly experienced with this configuration, but the individual does go through a great deal of spiritual growth and envolvement.

The lesson of this house polarity is how to balance the demands of the personal ego with the impersonal will of divine consciousness.

KEYWORDS: powerful ego, attractive, energizes others, self-centered, extremely sexual, develops strong moral values, confident, sincere, self-sufficient, joyful, attracts unique partner, union based on mutual recognition of individuality, needs outlets for sexual frustration, learns impersonal love through marriage.

Virgo First House—
Pisces Seventh House

With Virgo in the first house we seek perfection in our sexual identity. We look for a partner we can reform because it is difficult for us to tolerate imperfections in our ego-ideal. We are usually not happy during the first half of life, due to a tendency to attract lovers that are not really good for us. Once we realize this we can change our own identity structure to a level which is more compatible with reality.

Physical appearance, meticulous dress and grooming are especially important to this person. When he doesn't feel clean about himself he tends to sublimate his sex drive by rationalizing it as mental discrimination. Even when he is realistic, his standards are exceedingly high, and he would rather deprive himself of sex than feel that he is in any way lowering his ethical or moral values.

Some individuals with Virgo in the first house tend towards bisexuality and homosexuality in their never-ending search for the "perfect self-union." Asexuality, abstinence, and celibacy are also not uncommon with this placement. When the individual is heterosexual, the Virgo ascendant creates a sense of personal smallness in relation to the infinite nature of the Pisces Seventh House that is sensed through a partner. The individual tries to express compassionate service to a mate, who may well be either an escapist, an alcoholic, a chronic liar or tempermental artist, or just a very illusive individual who lives in dreams that are not founded in reality.

There may be a tinge of the "saintly" quality in the ego. The person sees himself as a reformer trying to sympathize with an apparent underdog. He thinks his partner is his "martyr-like" mission. Pisces is the sign of "The Christ," and any individual with a Pisces seventh house will bear his own personal cross in marriage.

The tremendous amount of effort he puts in to give form, structure, value and meaning to a swirling sea of illusion and confusion brings out the best in him. He may know at times that the task seems futile but he nevertheless experiences a growing consciousness of a higher form of love in himself merely by trying.

The lesson of this House placement is usually learned later in life, after the individual realizes the importance of balancing the concrete ideals of his ego with the heavy sacrifices he must make in order to be able to experience the mystical depth of emotional feeling that he is seeking.

KEYWORDS: discriminative, idealistic, nervous, crafty, disillusionment causes hedonism, sometimes asexual, bisexual, or homosexual, sex drive affected by physical appearance, sometimes frigid, natural unconscious piety, supportive in marriage, sensitive mate, reaches divine love through union.

Libra First House—
Aries Seventh House

With Libra in the first house, sex tends to mirror the needs of the mate. The individual has difficulty knowing who he really is, and he is usually in love with love. Often he goes through life with rose-colored glasses, imagining romance in many situations. He can fool himself as well as those around him by not wanting to see the reality of his relationships.

The sexual identity is a passive one needing encouragement from the mate's enthusiasm. Basic insecurities and fears of rejection lead the individual to seek a forceful and sometimes selfish partner who knows how to lead. The sensitive, gentle and kindhearted nature of the Libra ascendant is perfectly content to follow the right person.

With all the ethereal lightness of this placement, the Taurus eighth house that usually accompanies it makes the sex needs quite earthy and strong. The natural physical and spiritual beauty of this individual can, through sex, find a very special outlet for expression. Individuality and a sense of identity occurs through marriage because the Libra ascendant (being the natural sign of marriage) tends to make the individual feel like only half a person when life forces him to function only for himself. When the identity is focused towards "we" instead of "me," the natural inner beauty of this placement begins to shine in all its fullness. It is through the Aries seventh house that a sense of one-mindedness and the importance of a singular direction in life is established. Being highly sensitive, this individual will absorb any selfish qualities that the partner has. Instead of this being something negative, however, it helps to add drive and momentum to an otherwise passive ego.

On a sexual level, the individual wants to please his partner, but it is his partner that teaches him that he must also please himself.

The lesson of this house placement is to focus the passive ego through marriage while at the same time learn how to balance partnership through the impersonal self.

KEYWORDS: sensitive, peacemaker, sacrificial to partner, impersonal identity, tactful, aesthetic, lewd relationships, sometimes bi-sexual, unconscious sado-masochistic complex, youthful mate, energetic sexual partner.

Scorpio First House—
Taurus Seventh House

This is the strongest sexed house placement in the zodiac. The fixed and determined nature of Scorpio and Taurus always draws its strength from sex desire. Even if the person is on the path of spiritual attainment, transformations through sexuality become the essence of the way. Sex sharpens the intuitive and instinctive nature, bringing out a keen though often silent personality covering a great deal of personal depth.

While peering into the innermost secrets of another, this person will cleverly mask the motivations of his own ego. This occurs because he does not really believe that others are capable of understanding life the way he sees it. His ideas, attitudes and actions come from a level that is basic, uninhibited, blunt, and amazingly real.

He tends to stalk his sexual targets, much like an animal looking for its prey. If married, he may have love affairs because he tends to use sex to confirm the correctness of his motivational outlook on life. Rather than brooding over minor things wrong in a marriage, he would sooner seek out secretive sexual partners to fulfill what he feels is lacking. His hectic battles within himself stem from the fact that his ego is an unconscious one. The torment of destroying himself and those close to him in an effort to reform all conditions in the world that are less than what his high ideals perceive is a constant source of irritation to him.

He may destroy himself to build another. Through marriage, he learns the values of endurance, patience, and the building of solid form that gives structure to what would otherwise be a very hectic lifestyle. His unconscious ego values sex over love, but the ego-ideals of his seventh house teach him exactly the opposite. Through many repeated experiences of destroying, only to have to rebuild, he slowly begins to understand how to merge the two into the meaningful blend that will bring him harmony.

He is a pleasure-seeker, and will seek a leisure-seeker as a mate. The greatest difficulties he experiences in relationships come from the way in which he deals with his possesive and jealous nature. He can literally destroy a marriage through suspicious projections of his own unconscious paranoia. If he learns how to direct his intensity he can transform his own ego as well as providing the depth his partner needs.

The lesson of this house placement is to learn how to transmute sexual energy into creative output, while at the same time realizing the value of solidly building new ideals.

KEYWORDS: intensely sexual, penetrating, secretive, lustful, sometimes obsessed, regenerative, sometimes bi-sexual, seeks unconscious truths, great fortune through union, sex-love conflict must be blended into harmony, perverse needs, lecherous tendencies, voyeurism.

Sagittarius First House— Gemini Seventh House

This person has plenty of sexual thoughts that do not necessarily manifest physically. The ego is identified with freedom and can use sex as a way of breaking out of bondage whenever it feels chained. When free, sex is not of such great importance to this individual. Instead, it is a symbol of other things.

The higher mind needs to feel that it is above the mundane. The sex that it experiences must in some way represent something more that what he feels others capable of understanding. He may not see love as something planned or preserved, but rather one of the adventures of life. As such he is very much a romantic, often chasing windmills, but nevertheless forever running from one adventure to another. This makes it difficult to be completely devoted to one partner. For this reason, along with a basic fear of commitment, individuals with this rising sign often experience divorce. What is interesting is that it is the idea of sexual opportunity rather than any real physical gratification from the act itself that keeps prompting the ego to diversify itself in many directions. There is an impatient need for spontaneity that keeps trying to break boundaries, transcend limits, and assure the individual that he is truly a free spirit.

When he does have a sexual fantasy, it is usually imagined in an outdoor setting which fulfills his need to feel that he is a part of nature. Marriage teaches him how to focus this interests in the vivid presence of the "Now" reality. The usually-inflated ego of Sagittarius tends to see things out of proportion, but it is the ego-ideals of Gemini in the seventh that focuses the perception of relationships between people that can help to bring this individual down to mundane reality. The self is always aware of the macrocosm while marriage is founded in the microcosm. Although the individual may have high-minded personal values that seem to touch universal truth, it is only through a marriage relationship that he can learn how to make them work. Both in the ego and in the ego-ideal, sex is more a curiosity instinct based on interest than it is a physical or emotional need.

The lesson of this house placement is the difference between seeing and being. The ego must learn how to express itself through the consideration of another, which helps to build the kind of marital understanding that will ultimately give the individual the truth he is seeking.

KEYWORDS: unsettled, free spirit, lacks emotional sensitivity, seeks spontaneous sexual experiences, bores easily, mental masturbation, attracts platonic relationships, dispassionate marriage, learning through partner, eclectic ego, divorce likely, mind-rapes others, difficult struggle with mortality.

Capricorn First House— Cancer Seventh House

With Carpicorn in the first, the individual seeks to establish a personal sense of sexual responsibility. He wants form, structure, dignity and self respect so he will try to avoid sexual behavior that violates these needs.

There is a need to hide himself so he puts up a wall between what he really feels and what he wants others to know. Self-pride and inhibitions are the building blocks of this wall, while his desire to defend himself against anything that might shake his security is the cement that holds it together. His sexual life may appear to be somewhat limited. Sex is somehow unconsciously linked with an inner obligation to the religious and moral ethics that he feels towards his God. While his interest in sex is not necessarily any less than any other sign, he realizes the importance of achieving and maintaining self-respect, not only for his own benefit, but also for the conservation and preservation of the principles he believes in.

Through marriage he learns how to get in touch with his emotions. Although his ego likes to wear a mask, his ego-ideal would really like to drop all the facades, come down to earth, and learn how to feel the interactions between himself and the person he loves.

This placement tends to make the individual "old for his age" during his youth for he is trying to live up to all he believes is expected of him. As he begins to observe the Cancerian traits of his seventh house, he slowly starts to reverse his patterns. Marriage brings out spontaneity with less planned responses, activities, and situations. He will always seek a mate who is highly affectionate, sensitive and warm, so he can ultimately realize these characteristics in himself.

Sex takes on a propriety that is not found in other areas in the zodiac. It becomes the important bond through which a family unit built on devotion is established.

The lesson here is for the matured ego to learn how to nourish a mate, and because of the warmth and sincerity that can be developed through marriage, receive in return the building blocks which establish its sense of value and purpose.

KEYWORDS: restricting, sober, sexually-repressed, inhibited, poor sense of timing, protective, strong sense of superego, worries over mate, sensitive to partner's sexual needs, dutiful, grows through marriage, fears of letting go, oedipal conflicts, immature partner needs evolvement.

Aquarius First House—
Leo Seventh House

With this placement, there is a great deal of sexual curiosity. The identity is constantly changing as the individual personally experiences an impersonal consciousness. Every time he thinks he finds himself, he discovers a new pathway that leads him searching again. He is an experimenter, but because this configuration is usually accompanied by Virgo in the eighth, his sexual instincts are more mental than physical. By knowing about other people's sexual adventures he can feel that he is part of something that extends beyond his own personal smallness. In a way, he often teases himself, much like the proverbial donkey following the carrot that he has placed in front of his own nose.

For all his mental curiosity, he nevertheless tends to be sexually cool. His approach is mechanical, scientific, clinical and seeking. This makes his sexual behavior less humanistic and more research-oriented. He can be original, kinky, spontaneously adaptable to almost anything and in some cases bi-sexual or homosexual. This is all a product of his need for discovering who he is.

Marriage teaches him how to pull the loose ends of his personality together so he is able to find constructive and meaningful purpose to all he experiences. This is one of the few zodical placements where it is almost impossible for the individual to find his personal self without marriage. The Uranian energies that influence the ego are too erratic for this person to sense a oneness with his existence. The demands of the Leo seventh house, however, enable the individual to focus his desires to give. Thus he can find (through marriage) the sense of purpose that his ego-ideal needs in order to make use of all of the existential possibilities he senses in the world.

His mate is usually highly-sexed, but with a good sense of command and perspective. The scattering herd of thoughts in the Aquarius ascendant find their shephard to follow via the marriage.

The lesson of this placement is that freedom of self is achieved by selflessly serving a mate whose high standards and principles help to elevate the consciousness of the impersonal ego.

KEYWORDS: original, futuristic, independent, sexual experimentor, curious nature, sexually adaptable, sometimes bi-sexual or homosexual, misunderstood, need to fulfill others, cursader-type ego, aloof impersonal behavior in intimate situations, needs an honorable partner, purpose through partner, self-worth through marriage, sexually-demanding mate.

Pisces First House— Virgo Seventh House

This is the most loving and mystical ascendant in the zodiac. The individual identifies with the pure essence of romance. He lives in a dream of love without boundaries. When either Libra or Scorpio in the eighth house accompanies this placement, the person has to cope with the problem of losing himself through sex. He can easily dissipate his energies by trying to please another too hard. This occurs when he has little confidence in himself or he doesn't feel that his sexual ideas will be accepted. Timidly afraid of being judged for his sexual interest, he may try to hide in the mist of his imaginative Piscean sea.

The romantic identity stems from his living in a world of pictures, movies and fantasies that center around great beauty and periods in history when fanciful clothing, chivalry and gentle courtships were important. His mystique and shyness absorbs others into his sexual vibration. Whether male or female, this person is usually hauntingly enticing, with just enough of a cloudy haze around him to leave others in constant suspense. Sexually he can be very loving and giving as he tries to create some vague gossamer impression of romantic intrigue. With this placement, the individual's conception of personal love often touches the infinite.

Marriage helps to bring the ego down to earth by adding a dimension of clarity to all that he perceives. Through his mate, he is able to find order in himself. Thus, he begins to sense that he is part of something tangible rather than simply a floating essence.

On a sexual level, the Pisces ego is overly diffused and self-deluded. Through the ideals of the Virgo seventh house, however, the individual can learn the positive values of limiting his sexual expression. He acquires knowledge which teaches him how to discriminate. Through discrimination he eventually comes to discard those dreams that are unrealistic and directs himself towards those that will bring him fulfillment.

KEYWORDS: intriguing, mystical, erotic, sometimes masochistic, self-sacrificing, gentle, compassionate, smooth, illusive, loses self in dreams, can be bi-sexual, sometimes perverse, discriminating partner, idealizes mate, strict marital relationship, sadistic experiences, achieves realism through marriage.

6. The Second and Eighth Houses

The second house symbolizes all the things, ideas, attitudes and people that an individual holds dear in his value system. Values are a possession. They represent all that makes a person important to himself. Because of this, the second house is the storehouse or "cupboard" from which a person can feed others by giving. When this is seen on a sexual level, the second house represents what one gives to a partner during the sexual experience.

Sex is more than just the physical interplay between individuals. There are always exchanges (or gifts) that are shared. In fact, one of the primary reasons why one person feels a sexual desire for another is because there is something to be given and something to be received. This "something" may be an idea that one has looked for, or an answer to a question that one has been asking for a long time, or it may be the surfacing of unconscious strength, power, or direction in life. Literally it could be any number of different things. The important point is that each individual can be both a giver and a receiver as a result of every sexual experience. Those experiences in which nothing is given or received beyond mere physical gratification usually leaves a person feeling empty, frustrated and entangled in the same unrequitted desires that brought him to the experience. But those experiences which include this interplay of giving and receiving are extremely rewarding to both partners.

People have sexual patterns, and regardless of how many experiences they actually have there is a strong tendency for these patterns to repeat themselves. It is through this symbolic repetition of expressing second house values that a person learns what his greatest worth to others is. To understand how the polarity between the second and the eighth house works, we have to understand the basic essence of Taurus (the natural second house) and Scorpio (the natural eighth house).

Taurus collects matter to form substance, while Scorpio eliminates all that is no longer useful in order to achieve transformations. The second house of values is really based on what an individual has formed in matter. An individual's value system is very much a measure of his substance. The sense of giving that comes from the second house is a product of how a person proves that his value system is substantially valid. Through the Scorpionic nature of the eighth a person transforms his values. By eliminating all that is not valid he is able to receive the fulfillment of his deepest needs and he learns to accept other's values as well. The Taurus rulership of the second house shows the naturally possessive relationship between an individual and the things he stands for. At the same time, the Scorpio rulership of the eighth house shows how much our values undergo turbulent transformations because of others.

Traditionally, the eighth house is the house of sexuality. Thus, if we are to understand both the second and the eighth house in terms of polarity, we must see how sexuality and personal values are functions of each other. It is through sexuality that an individual experiences his most intimate contact with the substance of another. Thus, he can measure his ideals, principles, and values against what he absorbs from his sexual partner. There is no question that sexuality transforms values. The converse of this is also true. Values have a strong effect on a person's sexuality.

Through the depths of the eighth house an individual can also learn how to receive from his inner self. This secret house holds within its confines the most private intimate sexual thoughts and desires that an individual has. These are usually so deeply locked away that it almost seems like another world in comparison to the every-day reality one lives in. People can experience sex and still not be in touch with the unconscious depths of their eighth house needs.

One of the outstanding reasons for this is that since it is also the house of criminal drives and activities, there is a tendency to experience a great deal of guilt in terms of truly admitting to oneself the baseness of sexuality in its most raw form. Somehow the criminal associations in this unconscious house link up with one's deeply rooted concept of personal "sin" and cause latent or unconscious inhibitions that an individual might not even be aware of.

To truly understand one's sexual needs the problem of a dualistic identity structure has to be understood. There may be many facets of personality working at the same time in everyone. Nevertheless, there is usually a definite double identity structure that is clearly definable. One identity is made up of what we are taught by parents, teachers, the books we have read. This identity contains many compromises, for it is largely formed through the superego; that part of us that is formed because we want the acceptance of our society. Because of this, it does not completely reflect the way we truly are.

There is a second identity that is not influenced in this way. It comes from what psychology calls the "id" or our innate basic instincts. This identity is only found if one asks oneself the question, "How might an individual think, feel and act if he were not concerned about parental disciplines, religious taboos, society's acceptance, and the general weight that the entire superego imposes on him?" In other words, if we could be and do anything we wanted, what would we be like and what would we do? This is the instinctual part of us that is often neatly covered in order to guarantee our semblance of respectability in the eyes of others. In order to do this, however, we create so many buffers that we don't really put ourselves in full touch with this basic primevil force that drives us. To reach this we would have to imagine that there truly is nobody else in the world. There is really no superego force inhibiting our desires except that which we imagine. Once we realize this, we can begin to understand ourselves on a pure level. And, it is from this very essence that the seeds of our natural instinctual needs arise. Where the second house carries the collected values that we personalize for our own, the eighth house discards them so that we can find ourselves without shackles of having to live up to outer-world expectations. This is why sexual expression, when it is confronted on its most basic instinctual level, is such a release of pent-up tensions. It frees us from the boundaries of parents, education, religion, society and its taboos and gives us a few moments when we can really be in touch with ourselves.* It is in these moments that we almost feel like we are stepping from one world into another. And, in fact—we are! For many the change is difficult, for they try to stay cognizant of the fact that afterward they have to come back and face the mundane world again. In essence, they must be able to respect themselves once more in terms of the great superego force they feel in it.

When an individual is truly in touch with his eighth house experience, he goes through identity changes. As the sexual unconscious is allowed to surface and express itself freely, all of the unreal values that he considers to be part of himself somehow miraculously disappear. Instead he becomes in touch with his very real sexual identity that makes him feel whole, complete and full, but which he also knows society will never truly accept. Herein lies the conflict that individuals experience constantly. Still, it is through this conflict that the self becomes regenerated as the surfacing of new values directly from the unconscious takes the place of old ones that are being given to others.

Aries Second House— Libra Eighth House

With Aries in the second house, the individual brings his own sense of oneness to sexuality. He gives youthfulness and vitality to his sexual partner along with a sense of making new beginnings. In this way, he regenerates others by teaching them how to take on challenges.

His greatest gift is the extent to which he values independence. From this, his sexual partners learn how to be unique individuals. The spontaneity of this placement symbolizes the manner in which he teaches others how to trust their initial instincts.

With all the Arian values, this person seems to unconsciously need the indecisiveness of others. Through the Libra eighth house, a

---

*To understand the reality of the "moment," see Martin Schulman, *Karmic Astrology, Vol. 4, The Karma of the Now* (York Beach, ME: Samuel Weiser, 1978).

balance is created between values that are highly subjective and those impersonal values which are more objective. As the person see-saws between his second and eighth house, a tendency to become a sexual chameleon may manifest vascillating between being sexually gentle and loving one time and quite defensive another. Sometimes, this person has to be led to sexuality in order to learn how to express all the love that comes from the unconscious levels of the eighth house. The basic inconsistancy is that Libra not only experiences his own unconscious, but also the changing unconscious desire of others. As a result, this individual is not always sure what urges are springing forth from him and what urges are coming from others. It is for this reason that his strongest drive is to be able to merge with another so that whatever occurs in the unconscious (from wherever its source might be) he can still feel love's oneness within himself. He needs complete sexual surrender and union in order to be fulfilled. Any sexual nuances short of this do little to complete the emptiness he experiences from an unconscious that leaves itself halfway open to another at all times.

His love is gentle, his understanding unique, and his ability to balance his partner's needs are unparalleled by any other sign in this placement.

The lesson in this Aries-Libra polarity is to learn how to give of one's self so that the deep unconscious need for love can be realized.

KEYWORDS: resourceful, primitive desires, dreamy sexual life, eager for experience, highly sexed, gives strength to partner, child-like instincts, sometimes imagines both sexual roles, seeks gentle sexual partners, ego-centering through sex.

Taurus Second House— Scorpio Eighth House

This is the natural placement for the second and eighth house. Here the individual is able to bring a strong sense of solidity and security to his sexual partner. He knows how to build from the bottom up, and makes an excellent lover for anyone who has difficulty finding stability. Highly practical, he values sound, down-to-earth reasoning ability. He treasures patience and understands that things of great worth take time and dedication to achieve. All of these thoughts are transfered to a partner during the sexual experience. In fact, this individual may even want sex more than other signs because of the great need to see another as an extension of the self.

The Taurus second house brings a great deal of love and warmth to the sexual experience. The comfort and feelings of safety or security that are given to a partner are not easily forgotten. Perhaps the strongest gift here is the instinctive sense that there is a goal to work toward. From this gift, the partner begins to understand the real meaning of the continuity of feeling, which is the foundation of any enduring relationship.

The Scorpio eighth house allows the unconscious to surface in its fullest form. Here, through its natural rulership, the person needs to learn that a true confrontation with the real depths of his sexuality is absolutely necessary if all of the other areas in life are to flow smoothly. The unconscious drive is intense, and if it is not allowed to express itself, the person can spend years feeling anger and resentment. However, when the deep sexual needs are explored, transformation of values can occur. The Taurus second house is so rooted in holding onto what was once comfortable that no regeneration at all would occur if not for the hectic sexual experiences that churn the unconscious because of the tumultuous upheavals of the Scorpio eighth house.

Transformation is an extremely difficult process which takes place over a period of many years and through many different experiences. When sexuality becomes the battlefield of the ego transforming itself there is a strong likelihood for sado-masochism, perverse needs, and intensely unsatisfied desires to permeate the lifestyle. There is an innate crudeness to this placement that keeps an individual in touch with his base roots until the transformation of the ego is completed. From that point on, sexuality starts to take on a finer essence as it truly begins to reflect the desires of the higher self.

The lesson here is that by powering another's desires, one keeps inviting the changes that transform the self. Staying in control of the desire nature influences the speed at which changes in the self take place, and ultimately becomes the foundation for establishing the real meaning in life that the higher ideals of the Scorpio eighth house is truly seeking.

KEYWORDS: strong physical magnetism, affectionate, warm, possessive, protective, jealous, sensitive to partner's sexual needs, devotional, seeks to strengthen emotions through sex, intense desire nature, sado-masochistic expression, keenly perceptive, extremely personal, seeks the metaphysical meaning of life through sexuality.

Gemini Second House— Sagittarius Eighth House

Here the individual has a dualistic value system. On the surface this appears to present a great deal of confusion. In essence, however, it teaches the individual that there are two sides to everything. As one learns the value of objectivity, the sense of security that is so often sought in life yields to a greater understanding of the yin and yang values that must be handled every day. There may be a great deal of role-switching with this placement as the entire idea of sexuality takes on the form of being a learning experience. The person values knowing how the partner feels, all that the partner is experiencing and even how he or she compares with others he knew in his past.

This place is excellent for learning the lessons of impersonal love, because every time the sex partner exaggerates the closeness of a relationship, the individual with Gemini in the second will back away. He tries to keep the relationship intact while also remaining somewhat free. Since both Gemini and Sagittarius have to do with the mind, this polarity shows the way an individual transcends the lower mind through sex. The unconscious needs of the eighth house are always somewhat "larger than life." Desire may be difficult to control as the individual keeps finding the need to expand his sexual horizons. Without care and wisdom this placement can cause a person to become sexually jaded at a young age. The unconscious is usually seeking such a wide variety of experiences, that after a time, very little seems new. Then he must confront the fact that he is not really sure what he wants from life.

When balanced, however, this is one of the rare individuals in the zodiac that experiences the supreme joy of sexuality. It brings him to a broad understanding of nature and the eternal oneness of all he is.

The tendency to roam and wander leads this person to keep seeking excitingly unique sexual partners. It is not so much the physical act of sex itself that is important, as is the series of different adventures that these partners represent. The needs of the Sagittarius eighth house are geared towards overcoming boredom. Obviously this is a difficult placement for marriage. But it does allow the individual to reach his higher mind through sex.

By giving the gift of dual values, which enables the partner to objectively see both sides of something, this person receives the sense of freedom that he seeks. The lesson here is that sexuality can bring a higher unity to the multiple divisions in life perceived by the native. In a way, the Gemini-Sagittarius polarity is much like a triangle with its two opposing base points in the second house, pointing to the apex of truth in the eighth. The questions that the individual always asks himself are resolved by absorbing the more expansive values of his sex partner.

KEYWORDS: inconstant, great mental resources, stimulates partner, gives objective dualities to partner, role-switching, tendency to become dependent, great regenerative power through sex, difficulty in marriage, insatiable appetites, needs romantic partner able to provide variety, reaches higher mind through sex, ideally seeks sexual honesty.

Cancer Second House— Capricorn Eighth House

In this placement an individual spends a great deal of energy nourishing and strenghtening his sexual partner. He may be constantly concerned with how his partner feels and may try to put himself in her place to be sure that he is getting the right feeling across. This is one of the most giving second house positions. The individual tries to fill all the gaps that he senses his partner missed in childhood. He may try to be somewhat of a surrogate parent, giving roots, rules, boundaries, encouragement and strength to the one he loves.

Sometimes there is a tendency to attract waifs and strays that have no sense of home. Because he can sense a lack of stability he may try to give what he feels will establish a good emotional foundation for his sexual partner. Long enduring close relationships where he can share values of reliability and dependability are most appealing to him.

Through these he tries to build a safe haven with his partner. In most of his relationships, the love he gives will center around foods, wines, building things, fixing up apartments, etc. He is building and nourishing his sexual partner with an inner sense of security that goes much deeper emotionally than the outer manifestations show.

Sex is important here, as the Capricorn eighth house indicates committment with reason, serious purpose, and working toward some important goal. During the younger years, the unconscious tends to be locked up either because of childhood training, religious mores, or past-life karmic reasons* which make him feel that sex is something that has a certain amount of hidden guilt attached to it.

The sexual needs, then, tend to have barriers that the individual must learn how to break if he is ever to find himself. Once he does, sex becomes one of the most important areas in his life. He analyzes it and manages his life through it, and by seeing what kind of sexual experiences help to point him in the direction of his goals learns what experiences detract him from them. He can be one of the few people who eventually gain control of their unconscious drives and learn how to manage them so they become a neatly-fitting part of the rest of his existence.

For all of the nourishing of emotions that he gives through the second house, he also needs feedback that his sexuality is mature. The more he gives, the more he reaffirms his own sense of progress. Although he likes to experience the earthy qualities of Carpicorn, he nevertheless needs sexual partners who can respect him. His biggest conflict is that while his personality desires sexual respectability, he also needs strongly lustful experiences in order to build form for other creative areas in his life.

The lesson of this placement is that by giving emotionality to sexual partners who lack the ability to express their feelings openly, he receives the sense of propriety and dignity that comes from conserving sexual privacy. The walls of inhibitions that he may run into in a partner are exactly what he needs to establish himself.

KEYWORDS: warm, sensitive, affectionate, easily aroused, gentle, nourishes partner, enthusiastic, seeks emotional committment,

---

*See, *Karmic Astrology, Vol. 1 The Moon's Nodes and Reincarnation*, Martin Schulman, publ. Samuel Weiser Inc. N.Y. 1975 (pps 35-38, 70-72)

protective of partner, concerned with sexual aesthetics, settings, moods, inhibiting childhood, barriers to overcome, needs crude sexual experiences, sexually secretive, grows through practical partner, sometimes sexual power struggles, oedipal distortions, unconsciously desires sexual respectability, sexual fantasies from past periods in history.

Leo Second House— Aquarius Eighth House

With this placement, the individual gives his sex partner a strong sense of ego-value. He is attracted to people who don't know their creative worth; as a result, they feel aloof to all that life has to offer. His partners have preferences that run the gamut from the weird to the bizarre, and it is his function to bring some kind of dignity and pride to the sexual experience. To achieve this, he tries teaching another how to be more creative.

The Leo second house has much to give, and is both generous and romantic. The individual must first feel that his efforts are worth it and when he does he can give a great deal of power and control to a sensitive partner who may lack both. He must feel that he is also dominating the sexual experience. This he does by taking over the ego-role of his partner in addition to his own. He is able then to surface all the grandiose dreams that the partner had. He is able to bring a sexual partner to a higher level so she can expect more of herself and begin to feel the reality of actually achieving expectations.

Through the Aquarius eighth house, the range of experiences is exceedingly wide. In some instances there may be an unconscious urge for bi-sexual or homosexual relationships. The curious nature of Aquarius, blended with its thirst for adventure, leaves the unconscious open to many different channels at the same time. At times during the life, when this becomes too much for the individual, he may purposely throw himself into periods of abstinence or celibacy just to be able to detach himself enough to regroup his energies.

This is one of the few zodical placements that make an individual susceptible to rather strange sexual experiences. These may stem from what the unconscious emanates and what the conscious mind will not accept personal responsibility for, or they may happen because the person leaves himself too open on unconscious curiosity levels. More than any other sign in the eighth house, this individual goes through constant sexual changes. However he feels about his sexuality one year, it is likely that he will feel entirely different the next. The year after that, he may come up with new attitudes that seem to bear little relation to feelings he had previously. As we come closer to the Aquarian Age, these individuals should be observed considering that they may be sexually ahead of their time. Some of the ideas they express may be the foundations of future societies.

The Leo-Aquarius polarity always symbolizes the conflict between the personal and impersonal will. Here in the second and eighth houses, the individual is learning that what he personally wills for his sexual partner may bring him to the diversification of impersonal experiences. He can transform his ego-values into a broader cosmic understanding of a reality that he does not own.

KEYWORDS: great resources, dominates partner, attentive, loyal, creative values, needs sexual independence, keen curious nature, strongly regenerative, explorer, sexual needs constantly changing, sometimes bi-sexual or homosexual, personally moralistic, strange or kinky experiences, need to experience sexual contradictions, impersonal partner.

Virgo Second House— Pisces Eighth House

With Virgo in the second house, the individual has high ideals. Sometimes these may be unrealistic or impractical, but because this is the house of possession, he holds onto them. He tries to teach others to put borders and boundaries in their lives in order that they can better establish what it is they truly want.

This is a difficult position for marriage since the person inwardly expects more than what is realistically feasible. In sexual exploits, there is a tendency to look for that part of a partner that can be seen as "perfect." The strongest resource of this placement is clearmindedness, coupled with the ability to know how to put pieces of a puzzle together in order to pinpoint an illusive answer. Through sexuality, he helps his partner learn how to clarify thoughts and ideas so that vaguely obscured notions can become crystallized. His gift of love is reason and sensibility—a rare quality indeed in a world that often views love as undefinable and illogical.

The Pisces eighth house symbolizes the intuitive stream of consciousness that this individual receives from others through sexuality. He learns about romantic sensuality that somehow touches the infinite, and manages to find partners whose great depth and insight show him the cosmic meaning of sex. He does not like rough sexuality, but rather the smooth Neptunian experiences that harmonize his body and give him a feeling of being able to transcend time and space.

One of the difficulties in this placement is that the individual is extremely sexually sensitive to others and too much sex with too many different people tends to confuse his unconscious to the point where he has difficulty knowing his values. In addition to this, the eighth house Piscean tendency to lose oneself through sex has to be carefully balanced through a selective discrimination regarding sexual partners to ascertain that their consciousness is compatible to him. Pisces is the sign of the Soul. The sexual needs of the eighth house are always felt as part of a continuous stream of life's cosmic current. As such, the person's romantic imagination is able to see sexuality as an integrated part of everthing else that is. He can understand the forces of nature through sexuality as he comes in contact with the divine essence of reality. One day, he may receive glimpses of the Christ Consciousness through the compassion-blessed wisdom that is inherent in this very special placement.

The lesson of this Virgo-Pisces polarity is that by giving the values of clearmindedness and ideals of perfection, the individual can receive glimpses of the infinate from his sexual partner.

KEYWORDS: perfection seeking, high ideals, rigid values, strict realist, clearness, receives expanded consciousness through sex, compassionate partners, very sexually sensitive, clean-conscious, mystical attractions, sex increases perception of life, seeks union through Soul love.

Libra Second House—
Aries Eighth House

With this placement the individual brings his values of balance to the sexual experience. Often these include thoughts and feelings he has internalized from others. He can be extremely loving and giving; having a natural instinct to put the needs of his lover first, without truly considering his own gratification. If it is within his power to do so, he will give whatever it is he feels his partner needs. To do this, he will even create imbalances in himself. This makes him an extremist with a great deal of yin and yang in the expression of his own desires. He is always seeking the center of the road for his partner. He tries to teach his partner the value of harmony.

The second house is the house of desire and Libra is the sign of the eastern philosophy of "non-desire." This individual is levelling off excess desire in his partners. He tends to seek partners who are highly sexed. This is convenient for him because his basic nature is to allow another to initiate the act so that he doesn't really have to come out of his shell. While the partner is expending a great deal of energy to bring him out of himself, he keeps trying to convey the idea that it is love and not sex that makes a relationship valuable. A balance of energy is created and Libra has given its gift of harmony.

The unconscious needs of the Aries eighth house point in the direction of raw sexual expression on primitive levels. Sexual experiences always have the test of conquest in them. Lust, narcissism, exhibitionism and sex for power all come into play with this placement. What is really occurring is that the Libra-like values of the second house are so gentle and attracted to harmony that the individual constantly doubts his sexual power. Thus, through the Aries eighth house, the ego tries to prove its worth. It is not so much the completion of the act that is important as the realization that the individual is capable of action. The entire self-identity structure is strongly centered around how successful the individual can be in the initiation of sexual experience. He goes through spontaneous attractions in order to transcend the restrictions of society that keep him from being himself. The tighter these restrictions, the more tempting is the challenge for him to use this avenue as a means of proving his selfworth.

For this individual, sexuality symbolizes regenerative beginnings. He confronts his unconscious aloneness in the depths of a universe he can sense but does not fully understand. From this he developes the oneness which ultimately becomes his sense of self-esteem.

The lesson of this placement is that only through the giving of love on an impersonal level can the individual find his real identity. The more this person gives of his values—beauty, harmony, peace and love—the more he receives the knowledge of who he is.

KEYWORDS: generous nature, loving, artistic resources, idealistic, creative but not overly imaginative, values harmony, finds identity through highly active sexual life, spontaneous attractions, short-lived affairs, tends to project self-distortions to partner, sometimes unconscious bi-sexual desires, regenerates ego-strength through partner's resources, soothes mate, brings beauty to sex.

Scorpio Second House— Taurus Eighth House

This individual is highly sexed as well as being sexually possessive. His attitudes are basically honest. He holds within him one of the greatest gifts in the entire zodiac for he is able to help put his partner in touch with the unconscious. This is a truly remarkable experience, for most people are totally unaware of underlying motivations. We tend to go through much of life hiding our feelings and avoiding the instincts within us. We often wonder why we are not fully in touch with ourselves. When we are able to receive the gift of understanding the unconscious motivations, everything miraculously starts to become clear.

The individual with Scorpio in the second values destroying all that is old and archaic in another person's attitude makeup. Because of this, he may seem dangerous. Most people are extremely possessive of their attitudes. This individual can give his partner the impetus and strength of conviction to leave the old behind in order to make way for the new.

The Taurus eighth house creates a constant sexual urge. The

five senses are attuned to a strongly sensual and earthy nature. Among the sensitivities, his sense of touch and smell are the most highly developed. These play an important part in the sexual act, for they are an integral part of his telepathic and receiving system for understanding non-verbal messages. Not liking to rush sexual activity he lulls himself to the point that it becomes something to be savored. It is the appreciation of a rare wine. It is the reassurance of love at nature's divine core. And, he has all the time in the world, so as not to use up the experience before his cup is filled.

This placement is unquestionably the epitome of sexual love. The individual also has to learn how to balance himself so that he does not overdo something very beautiful.

The Scorpio-Taurus polarity always symbolizes destruction and building. Here in the second and eighth house, the individual is able to constructively regenerate his own values through the receiving of sincere sexual love. His intensity gives much depth to his partner, while in turn he receives new substance to the meaning in life that he is seeking. The lesson is that through giving the partner the energy for change through sex, stability in one's own creative values is achieved.

KEYWORDS: intense desire nature, aggressive, sometimes hedonistic, compelling, obsessive, jealous, powerful lovers, capable of very deep insights through sexuality, gives partner the gift of perception of the unconscious, great regenerative power, communication through body-touching, deep, full feelings, gives sexual depth to receive constancy in love.

Sagittarius Second House— Gemini Eighth House

With Sagittarius in the second house, the individual values his freedom. He does not wish to feel inhibited by others. With Gemini in the eighth his keen interest in all forms of sexuality is more mental than it is physical. Ideas have to be communicated so that relationships can develop. Usually he attracts partners who experience different society-oriented sexual problems based on sexual fears and guilt. Through the gift of his Sagittarius second house, he can expand these ideas for his partner and free her from the shackles of unnecessary social bondage. He values the natural rather than the staid. He can be rather philosophical about sexuality, detaching himself from too much intimacy. He can convey the knowledge of how to "loosen up" the restraints that bound his partner in her childhood. He gives the gift of happiness.

The Gemini eighth house is particularly interesting for it symbolizes the development of the individual through the elementary school years. As a result, there tends to be immature sexual desires on unconscious levels. Sometimes, asexuality, bisexualtiy, homosexuality, mental masturbation and extended periods of frigidity occur. When they do not, the individual's unconscious sexual drive is usually based on some type of storybook fantasy that tends to remain undeveloped. He may like to keep his distance during sex. He may have desires to express what he feels but holds back because he worries about what his partner might think of him.

Taking on roles from books he read, he may imagine himself playing out a scene from some page, or a vignette from a movie that has struck his fancy. Physical sexuality is not as important as the idea that he is actually observing himself in what appears to be behavior that amazes his conscious self. Many people with this placement can only break through conscious inhibitions when they are able to talk during the sexual act. It is something the unconscious is crying out for, but they find it difficult to do. The deepest unconscious need here is for understanding both sides of sexual communication.

The lesson is the understanding of the interplay of sexual roles. The more impersonal truth the individual is able to share during the sex act, the more he is able to understand the nature of his place in a sexual relation. This is one of the most humane, kind and least possessive placements in the zodiac.

KEYWORDS: great resources, tends to test partner, values ideas, free-spirit, generous, seeks humane sex, values decency in partner, often rationalizes needs, sometimes sublimates physical sexuality into mental pursuits, youthful, kind, flirtatious, innocently inconstant, childlike unfulfilled sexual experiences, needs gentle sexual partners, sometimes unconscious bisexual or homosexual needs, periods of frigidity, voyeurism, curious of others sexual secrets.

Capricorn Second House— Cancer Eighth House

The value system takes many years to mature. When it finally does, the values are sound, practical, realistic and usable. The individual with a Capricorn second house is a "fantasy-breaker," cutting through what he sees as nonsensical illusions in order to help his partner realize things as they are. He values people who are less experienced than himself so that he can play the role of teacher. This helps confirm his own solidity.

Even with all the maturity of his value systems, he tends to be sexually possessive, collecting sexual partners much like a philatelist collects stamps. Each new love is the one that will be the most meaningful in his collection. Interestingly enough, it is he himself that gives his partners the meaning that he percives in them. The greatest gift he can give to his lovers is a sense of importance that helps them overcome whatever inadequacies they experienced in their childhood.

With all that the Capricorn second house gives through sexuality there is still a need to feel deep emotions through another. Capricorn tends to be rigid and dry, formed and established, in essence, a pillar of strength. The Cancer eighth house gives this individual the fluidity of sexual emotions that enable warmth to fill the solid house of Capricorn values. There may be a natural mothering instinct in the sexual partner. Even if the partner tends to be immature in other ways, much nourishment can be received from the Cancer-like giving that flows through this eighth house position.

Sexual imagination, creativity, and charitable sensitivities pervade the sex experience. There is much fantasy revolving around an unconscious desire to possess for the purpose of protecting future security. Many with this placement experience strong needs to act out a parental role. Interestingly enough, the unconscious often experiences feelings of infidelity after he has a child of his own. Somehow the unconscious needs reassurance that it has not lost its own childhood. It is not sexuality itself that the unconscious craves, but rather the regaining of mother love and on the surface these emotional needs may seem to have nothing to do with sexuality at all.

The Capricorn second and Cancer eighth polarity represents a peculiar syndrome in psycho-sexual development. The individual values parenthood and the family structure so much he must find ways of acting it out on a sexual level. At the same time, the realism inherent in the Capricorn value system needs to constantly reaffirm that he is in fact not the parent of his lover. After many experiences, this polarity ultimately develops into one of the most upstanding and moralistic positions in the zodiac.

The lesson is that the richness of sexuality is only possible when an individual allows himself to be vulnerable; vulnerability, in turn, is only possible when it is accompanied by a strong sense of security. Sex with committment, promise, and future goals is truly what this individual seeks.

KEYWORDS: possessive, steadies affections, practical, sexual teacher, builds partner within limits, capable of deep feelings through sex, sensitive partners, breast conscious, seeks vulnerability with security, possessiveness and dominating attitude often leads to divorce, attracted to younger sexual partners.

Aquarius Second House— Leo Eighth House

With Aquarius in the second house, this person values new and unique experiences, but due to the fact that Capricorn usually appears in the first, he may tend to hide himself, not really wanting others to know the way he feels. He may be highly curious and interested in a wide variety of sexual experiences; however, his Leo eighth house keeps him from too much careless abandon because of self-pride and ego-esteem.

Basically, he doesn't like the rules of society, for he feels they are too rooted in the past. Instead he seeks to find his values from the future. It is important for him to remain slightly impersonal in whatever he does, for the gifts he gives are easier for him to give on that level. He transmits the knowledge of limitless freedom of expression based on values that quite literally represent Joseph's coat of many colors.

With this placement there may be an unconscious interest in bisexuality and deviations of all kinds. The individual wants to understand how things work. This investigative kind of curiosity often puts him in a dilemma. He values what he does not yet know about, while at the same time, he realizes that society may not sanction his ideas. In both sexes there is a propensity towards secret love affairs. The position and aspects to Jupiter (which play a strong role in influencing the fourth quadrant in this horoscope) have to be considered in order to pinpoint this in any particular individual.

The Leo eighth house tends to make sexual experiences symbolic representations of the personal ego battling for command. By being sexually competitive, the individual's personal sense of willpower (needed for other areas in life) is able to be developed. Sometimes this placement leads to periods of celibacy, as the individual can dislike himself for indulging in any form of sexuality that demeans either himself or his partner. His desire for command and his need for morality and self-respect cause a conflict in him which makes it difficult to fully accept his need for sex. As a result, he may know what he wants and needs but has to find acceptable ways of getting it so he does not lose dignity in his partner's eyes. His greatest sexual fulfillment comes from his ability to express love with honor. Some with this placement seek lovers who remind them of the age of chivalry in an effort to preserve a sense of human dignity in an age where it seems to be a rare quality.

The balance between the Aquarius-Leo polarity is one of ideals and creativity. Aquarius dreams of the future, and since the future is never here and now, these dreams are often highly idealistic. Through sex, these ideals are molded as the fiery inspirational qualities of the Leo eighth house helps focus them in the confines of the present reality. As a result, the individual tends to give of his idealistic freedom-oriented values in order to learn how to develop realistic command over himself. Sex gives him energy, power, and self-respect when he is wise enough to follow his finer instincts.

The lesson in this placement is that the more one is impersonal about the value they give to another, the more strength they build within.

KEYWORDS: values freedom, curious, innovative, imaginative, unconventional, generous, impersonal value systems, limitless resources, tends to push sexual partners towards future, seeks sex with honour, deeply passionate, possessive partner, ego-strengthening through sex, silent jealousies, showy behavior, ego-strengthening through sex, power struggles with partner, chivalrous, meaningful intentions.

Pisces Second House—
Virgo Eighth House

With Pisces in the second house, the individual values compassion, romance, imagination, dreams, and everything that is slightly intangible. He is more sensual than he is sexual. In this sense, the dream of sexuality overrides the actual act, which never really seems to measure up to the ideal created in the imagination.

There is self undoing in this placement as the person constantly allows his possessions and values to keep slipping through his fingers. He does, however, place some emphasis on appearances, which keeps his dreams seemingly real.

On a sexual level, the gift he gives is the power of imagination and the strength of belief. This is extremely important to those who lack self-confidence or need reasons to justify existence. The self is always made subservient to the partner in order to help bolster the lover's ego. In many ways, the gift of the Pisces second house reflects divine love in human expression.

Where Pisces symbolizes service to others, Virgo represents service to one's self. This individual does much for himself by keeping his sexual ideals in tune with the principles that he feels are correct. He can either be discriminating or seek hedonistic adventure; if he chooses the latter, he will not be serving his higher self. The Virgo eighth house is a strongly moralistic placement. The individual not only has strong feelings about what is sexually correct for himself, but also for others as well. Some with this position will even judge the complete character of others because of what appears to be loose sexual behavior.

A certain amount of childhood inhibitions always accompany this placement. There is difficulty in relating intimately to members of the opposite sex due to fears of rejection and personal embarrassment about one's own sexuality.

A difficult psychological problem exists on two levels. First, the individual's value system (as symbolized by the Pisces second house) is nebulous, but he unrealistically expects specific ideals from others through the unconscious needs of his eighth house. Secondly, the unconscious drives are supposed to be raw and base for they stem from an individual's roots. As a result, he usually rationalizes much of his life avoiding the purification of his own carnal instincts by attributing them to others, instead of realizing that he truly is an instrument of perfected sexual love afraid of being crucified by the standards of his society.

The lesson of this placement is based upon the fact that values are a product of consciousness, and the more the individual gives of an unselfish consciousness, the more he receives the perfected ideals that the higher self is seeking.

KEYWORDS: sensuous, natural sense of beauty, considerate, compassionate, gentle, understanding, creative, giver of dreams, artistic, musical, sensitive to lover's needs, judgemental of other's sexuality, analytical of sexual movements, seeks honesty in sex, sometimes overly moralistic, clings to details, much sexual nervousness, quest for purer forms of sexuality, periods of asexuality, can be childlike or hedonistic, platonic tendencies, sometimes bisexual, needs perfect understanding from lover, rigid sexual ideas overcome through expanding consciousness.

7. The Third and Ninth Houses

These two houses represent an important polarity in the horoscope for where the third house shows how an individual integrates with another in a relationship, the ninth house indicates the way in which he experiences his relationship with his higher self. Traditionally, the third house represents the manner in which an individual comes close to people, ideas and events, i.e., the basic arena of integration with one's everyday world. The ninth house (under the natural rulership of Jupiter) can be used merely as an avenue of escape for it also symbolizes bachelorhood, as well as the unity of self with nature, and may influence a desire to be alone rather than in the company of others.

Both these houses (under the rulership of Mercury and Jupiter) represent states of mind. The third house holds within it the lower mind experiences that keep an individual in touch with his mundane reality. The ninth house is the key to one's spiritual experiences which lift our consciousness to a higher reality. In addition, both houses symbolize different kinds of learning.

There is no question that sexuality is a state of mind, and sex (in whatever form it occurs) is a learning experience. To understand this, we must consider that the third house rules the five physical senses of sight, hearing, touch, smell and taste; all of which play a pronounced role in sexual experiences. This house also rules the elementary school years, when primary learning tunes the senses to patterns they will follow in the future.

The ninth house symbolizes higher sensory communication and more evolved learning patterns. Where the third shows the way an individual tries to understand the connotative and denotative meanings of words, phrases and abstract language, the ninth house shows how we understand things through vibrational wavelengths. Often we know things, but we don't know how we know them. Much of this intuitive knowing comes from the ninth house because it is not dependent upon relationships to see things clearly. The yin and yang that occurs in third house dualities is resolved by the overview that the ninth house takes of the totality. From this totality, attitudes are formed, spiritual philosophies take the place of disconnected ideas, and the true values of sexuality (because the ninth is the second house from the eighth) begin to surface.

Let me digress for a moment. Every house in the horoscope can be seen as the result of the house that precedes it. The third house symbolizes the sexual thoughts and communication that results from one's own values (second house) as well as what one is able to give. The ninth represents the *results* of an individual's sexual needs. The communication that these two houses (of mind and ideas) symbolize contain a clear cut polarity. In the third house, we see all that one tries to communicate to another, while the ninth shows our personal philosophy. When we ask a person, "What do you think?" we are referring to the third house, but when we say to a person, "Make up your mind," we are directly touching ninth house qualities.

To understand these houses better, we must consider importance of consciousness as it is linked to sexuality. An individual's consciousness may be an outgrowth of *conscience*. Conscience is often put to its greatest tests because of sexuality! If we look at the process in reverse, sex is often the proving ground for the development of a clear conscience, which in turn results in an elevated and expanded state of consciousness.

In people who go through life without a clear conscience, the third house (of dualistic thought, conflicting ideas, and all of the effects of the condition we call lower mind) tends to actually "rule" the ninth.

When the sexual conscience is clear, the mind is better able to hold rulership over the third house. The yin and yang ideas of others are understood in terms of a higher truth emanating from an individual's impersonal consciousness.

To understand this in a sexual perspective all that one gives is a product of the past. All that one receives symbolizes the formation of the present and the development of the future. We tend to fear the unknown. The eighth house represents the unknown and the ninth house (of consciousness) is symbolic of the future growth that occurs when we can receive from the unknown. When this is possible we need not fear the future, for we are building a consciousness that is well prepared for it.

Sexual partners who are giving in nature contribute to each others future sense of security. Partners who do not give much tend to remain in repetitive patterns from the past.

Sex is not an isolated physical act. Physical sex involves combining your consciousness with anothers. An enhancement of awareness or a closing up that inhibits consciousness can take place. In our private moments when we think about the meaning of sex, we always relate it to consciousness.

The least rewarding sexual experiences occur when we experience sex with someone whose consciousness is far less developed than our own. The act leaves us feeling empty or disappointed. When we experience sex with someone who has a similar consciousness at a similar point in time and space, then the act is deeply fulfilling, richly rewarding, and becomes a springboard for more understanding and evolvement. People are definitely attracted to each other because of a need to grow. The level of awareness that exists in the ninth house may be difficult to verbalize and may be more easily transmitted silently through the sexual experience.

Sex, then, has a strong effect on one's mind. In the third house, it shows the way we integrate with society, while in the ninth it shows how we reach the higher self as well as how the development of consciousness plays a role in the evolution of the entire race.

Aries Third House—
Libra Ninth House

With this placement, sexual development may be quite mental. The individual strongly telepaths his desires as he communicates through his eyes. There is nothing subtle here for the need to see the completed act may be imagined or visualized immediately, even before the partner is aware of what is happening. The mental urgency of Aries bypasses the mystique and beauty of the experience. Interestingly enough, this individual tends to lose sexual interest as soon as he has proven to himself that it is possible to mentally subdue a partner who represents a challenge to him.

Sexual performance may be childlike—coming from neurotic fixations formed between age seven and fourteen. It is during these years that children are most interested in testing sexual worthiness by establishing acceptability to others. Whenever Aries appears in the third house, something is usually left unresolved at this stage of development. The adult communicates his desires intensely but does not really receive fulfillment because he may not understand he can by being more *receptive.*

The idea of *starting* a sexual experience is strongest in his mind. The rest of the experience—touching, the mystique, the act, the awareness that comes from it are all secondary. He may be in such a hurry to communicate that he forgets to listen or be receptive to his partner.

The Libra ninth house represents a rather paradoxical consciousness. There is the need for fairness and objectivity in the higher mind. Western consciousness seeks to achieve a one-minded decisiveness, while Eastern consciousness recognizes the yin and yang of opposing forces. Libra in the ninth puts the individual more in touch with the East than the West. He is able to see both sides of the truth, but may not be able to conceptualize one as being better or worse than another. On a personal level, relationships which are ruled by the opposition coming from Aries in the third are often too one-sided to flow easily.

The ninth house symbolizes attitudes, opinions and judgements that one must make in life as we discriminate between the influences that either alter or balance our path. With Libra here, it is difficult to make decisions about the important things in life. Libra sways first to one side, then the other; never really quite sure of where the center is. Because of this, sexuality may have more of an effect on his consciousness than it will on others.

In extended relationships, he may spend a great deal of energy balancing the values of his sex partner. In short relationships, or single sexual encounters, he tends to be somewhat selfish. Because of the particular qualities of the Aries-Libra polarity, he may learn about sexual expression through one-time initiatory experiences but he learns about love (Libra in the Ninth House) through higher-minded relationships that free his spirit by giving him union with his higher self.

KEYWORDS: flirtatious, aggressive, attracts youthful people, popular, energetic, autonomous, impatient, shows partner how to achieve self-esteem, confident, tries to balance sexual partner, mental masturbation, independent, initiatory, charitable, forgiving of partner's errors.

Taurus Third House— Scorpio Ninth House

With Taurus in the third house the physical senses are highly developed. The individual communicates through touching. The physical body remembers past illnesses and emotional traumas long after they are healed. The individual with Taurus in the third communicates by intuitively knowing just where and how to touch these different areas (which are in different locations with each sexual partner) and through his Venusian touching, communicates a great deal of healing love to his partner.

In effect he is a master at sexual and sensual communication. He can give as well as receive and his sense of smell is so highly developed that he will remember his partners by a "psychic scent," which is always uniquely individualistic to each person.

Because his communicative faculties are so well-developed he is an excellent lover on many levels at the same time. Perhaps what is most outstanding with this placement is the amount of tenderness he is able to give.

The Scorpio ninth house symbolizes a crusade through sexuality. It makes the person aware of how much occurs on unconscious levels and at the same time, how much he can use sex to transform his own attitudes. Thus, he can flow with anothers stream of consciousness because he knows it is a different stream that holds keys to doors he has not yet unlocked. And the inquisitiveness of the higher mind make him extremely anxious to find out what he does not yet know. He is a seeker after the great mystery of life, and through the Scorpionic nature of this ninth house, tries to understand the sexual nature of spiritual love.

The Taurus-Scorpio polarity is always somewhat possessive, jealous, and binding. It seeks a powerful meaning and fullness. The higher mind becomes focused through the lower mind so what the lower mind thinks must always be integrated. The intensity of Scorpio and the gentleness of Taurus must work together on these two mind levels if the individual is to see sexuality as a constructive and regenerative force in his life.

KEYWORDS: Sensuous, pleasure-loving, sensitive, sexual touching important, capable of deep caring, possessive thoughts, jealous, becomes attached easily, seeks truth and honesty, needs sense of sexual purpose, crusader instinct, much depth, insight, telepathic, intuitive, can be suspicious of partner's motivations, keenly perceptive, seeks enduring relationships, can be sexually obsessed, compulsive thoughts, powerful sexual habit patterns.

Gemini Third House— Sagittarius Ninth House

This is the natural placement for Gemini and Sagittarius. Communication begins with a great deal of mental and verbal activity. This individual can be sexually attractive. He is aggressive, and enjoys mental word games. He may be particularly sensitive and nervous with "goose-bumps" or "sweaty palms" occuring when he participates sexually.

When he tries to be aggressive he must overcome his fear of being rejected. He likes to see how each message is received before advancing further. His interest in sex tends to be more mental than physical. When he seeks gratification he may have to confront a coldness in himself, or he may ignore his partner's need for romance.

The Sagittarius ninth house can act as a balance for the consciousness or higher mind can perceive both sides of the issue. This helps the person to see a more full stream of consciousness. He can know people not only by themselves but also by their friends, the kinds of experiences they are having, the way they act and react to the circumstances in life, etc. And , the amazing thing is that he is able to know this almost effortlessly.

There is a thirst for experiencing all there is to sample in life. This manifests itself strongly on a sexual level as the individual's broad and open consciousness magnetizes him to relate best to those who understand his great need for mental freedom.

The lesson of Gemini and Sagittarius is found in the relationship between mind and experience. The more duality the individual sees through Gemini, the more he needs to experience (through Sagittarius) in order to resolve dichotomous thinking. The two sides of Gemini are not resolved by blending into oneness in Sagittarius, but rather by expanding the facets of duality for it creates an acceptance of all that could exist in the world. From this acceptance the great oneness of Sagittarius can then emerge.

KEYWORDS: versatile, sometimes platonic relationships, popular, attractive, mentally aggressive, youthful, playful, cold but understanding, witty, plays mental games, independent spirit, adventurous, restless, sensitive to sexual words, impatient, thirst for experience, plays roles, clever, flirtatious, needs harmonious partner.

Cancer Third House— Capricorn Ninth House

With Cancer in the third house, sexual communication takes place on an emotional level. The breasts and the stomach in the female, and the stomach in the male are the most physically sensitive areas. Whether male or female the individual needs sexual committment. Highly sensitive to his partner, this individual has a great need for intimate sexual expression, but he can only be that way after he knows his partner well. Trust does not come easily, for on a deep intuitive level he feels that many people are living behind facades.

Fulfillment comes only when sexuality is accompanied by a great deal of "tender loving care." There is always the ideas of need, an emotional pulling, a desire for comfort in a relationship. In a way, the individual sees relationships as insulators from feeling too much external discomfort from what is perceived to be an insecure world. Sexual vulnerability exists in direct proportion to the amount of security received from the partner.

The Capricorn ninth house makes the individual sensitive to attitudes, opinions, beliefs, and a level of consciousness that may remain unexpressed. An idea may be pondered for years as this individual tries to understand its ultimate value. He is a builder of consciousness. He does not want any of the bricks that form his temple to be misformed or the wrong size. He organizes his ideas, and formulates them into concepts, and from these concepts he builds a powerfully sturdy consciousness that is capable of buffeting him from many storms. One of the difficulties he must overcome is a higher-mind identification with guilt. Something in his makeup gives him a strong sense of conscience.

He tends to scrutinize others in order to see whether the plan for the unfolding of his understanding will be enhanced through their sexual intimacy with him, or whether he will tend to lose his track. Sexual experiences that take him off track make him feel guilty, because the most important thing is the powerful sense of responsibility he feels towards the ideas he stands for. In this respect he finds it difficult to understand those who appear aimless. He does not see life as a series of unrelated coincidences, but rather as a clearly defined and intergrated puzzle whose pieces may not appear to make sense, but nevertheless fit together perfectly as the passing of time makes their shapes more clearly defined. He sees meaning in everything, and each sexual experience is viewed as something from which there was a lesson to be learned; i.e., another piece in the puzzle that somehow makes life more tangible.

The real lesson of this placement is seen in the observation of the law of cause and effect. The initiatory qualities of the Moon-ruled Cancer third house symbolize all that emotional relationships can give birth to, while the Saturnian qualities of the Capricorn ninth show that emotional relationships give form to attitudes which help the individual mature. The emotions of Cancer become crystallized in Capricorn. If the person experiences constructive emotional relationships, then the form and structure of the higher mind is firmed up. If emotional relationships are unfulfilling, then the Capricorn attitude systems can become extremely negative. This placement shows how an individual's outlook on life can stem from what he experiences in an emotional relationship.

KEYWORDS: sympathetic, imaginative, sensitive, gentle, defensive, romantic, sensual, giving, teaches the quality of sustenance, seeks commitment, security-conscious, principled, needs responsible partner, sees life's lessons, must overcome guilt-ridden conscience, family-conscious, covert attitudes, sexually-monogomous instinct, possible incestuous feelings, finds purpose to life through positive relationships.

Leo Third House— Aquarius Ninth House

With Leo in the third house, sexuality stirs up the love emotion. This causes the problem of falling in love with too many sexual partners. Being highly romantic when he wants to communicate an idea, the individual may focus his attention around the drama of the act as it unfolds itself much like a play moving from scene to scene. He is highly imaginative and tries to take on the different roles that he feels will impress his partner who may symbolize his audience. The best way of communicating what he feels, thinks, and knows may be through a display of action, and he may want to mean more to his partner than she previously experienced with other lovers. The entire concept of romance sensitizes him.

One of the difficulties of this placement occurs when he tries to control sexual experience. When he feels that he has this control, he can communicate all he knows about creative loving, loyalty and devotion to his partner. When he does not feel this control, he may become philosophically detached backing away from the intimacy he really needs. Individuals who have this placemnt usually pick sex partners who have this difficulty to overcome as well.

With the intense sexual thoughts of Leo, a balance can still be achieved through the free consciousness symbolized by the Aquarius ninth house. The person is attracted to ideas that transcend established thought patterns. In fact, he seems to have little pattern at all for he is quite liberal in his attitudes. He believes in a "live and let-live" lifestyle. In intimate communication he may feel the crusader instinct and try to reform another. He may feel that his sense of right and wrong can be helpful to the person he loves. He never loses sight of his understanding that things can be different without one being necessarily better than another.

On a sexual level, he wants to understand his partner's attitudes. He will never judge his partner for the idea of judging is against all that he represents as a humanitarian. His sexual experiences may change him a great deal as he bounces from one extreme to another. There are times in life when he needs to do this for it helps him to balance himself. The Leo third house makes him feel powerful, but the Aquarius ninth house brings the silent realization that he is but a small speck in a world so large that he could only conceive of a portion of it at a time.

The lesson of this placement lies in the balancing of the personal will with the universal will. Even an individual can dominate a relationship, he must nevertheless confront the universal reason of what goodness he is adding to the world by doing it.

KEYWORDS: magnetic, popular, creative, powerful, cheerful personality, desires command in relationships, romantic to a fault, teaches partner the idea of devotion, fair as an outgrowth of generosity, understanding, crusading attitudes, competitive, flamboyant, responsible.

Virgo Third House— Pisces Ninth House

With Virgo in the third house, the individual experiences fears of expressing himself fully to the opposite sex. His concept of relating has been slow in developing during early school years, and he may experience some barriers that are difficult for him to break.

Sex is often most gratifying when it is a feeling rather than a thinking experience, but with Virgo here, the individual spends most of his energy analyzing his own acceptibility in a relationship. If Aquarius in the eighth house accompanies this placement the individual may either have some bi-sexual tendencies or a detached attitude towards sexuality. This attitude can keep him from feeling intimately self-involved. Instead, he may observe himself and his partner as though he were a third person watching from a safe distance.

Often sex makes this individual nervous, for he may have difficulty understanding what is expected of him. His communicative abilities become frustrated for he is not the same person with his clothes off as he is with them on. Once he feels that he has lost his composure, it becomes almost impossible for him to flow with the experience. Instead, he keeps trying to regain his "mental set." What he does communicate to a partner, in spite of this, is the idea that one should not lose oneself in sexuality, but instead always retain a strong sense of personal clearness.

The Pisces ninth house gives the individual the opportunity of experiencing a very beautiful and rich consciousness. Although much of what he believes is based on his imagination and the fairy tales that seem to constantly swim through his head, he is one of the few individuals that can experience a sense of peace in his higher mind. So subtle are the changes in his thought patterns, and so smooth is his flow that others wonder how he appears to be so free amidst all the harsh vissicitudes of life. The answer is simple. He stays in his "Mother Goose" book all the time and manages to see everything in life as part of one of the stories he is living through at the moment. As simple as this kind of consciousness seems to be, there is something deeply mystical about it, for although he always appears to have his head in the clouds, he somehow knows the correct answers to what others have literally racked their brains searching for.

On a sexual level, he experiences the trip down "The Yellow Brick Road," "Peter Pan," "The Wizzard of Oz," sometimes even the wicked "witch" who does terrible things to people. All of these characters are very real to him. Perhaps the greatest enlightment he reaches comes when he discovers that there really is no "Boogie Man."

This Virgo-Pisces polarity is a particularly difficult one to balance because what the higher mind knows the lower mind cannot easily express. The finite quality of intimate personal relationships through the Virgo third house is difficult to synchronize with the infinite cosmic awarenesses which may create sweeping changes in the attitude systems of the Pisces ninth. Sometimes sexual expression seems mechanized, particularly when the individual views himself only through his lower mind. Often there is a childlike quality that refuses to assume sexual responsibility. When these two signs and houses are balanced, however, the individual has the opportunity of integrating his lower mind thoughts with a higher reality.

KEYWORDS: nervous, analyzes relationships, timid, rigid thought, frustrated, possible bi-sexual feelings, seeks perfect sensitivity in a partner, fragile, sometimes overly moralistic, judgemental, childlike, highly imaginative, mystical knowledge, great spiritual beauty, seeks a perfect relationship.

Libra Third House— Aries Ninth House

With Libra in the third house, the individual tries to understand a balance of intimacy in all relationships. He may even put himself out of balance if it means creating peace within the person he wants to relate to. At times he can be extremely childlike, sublimating his sexual nature for the idea of a milder or less intense relationship; for his thoughts tend to center around a goal of establishing harmony with another.

Through a variety of different sexual experiences, he learns that the more he tries to center others, the more he loses his own center. This presents a peculiar conflict to him, for Libra does not like to do things alone and needs relationships more than any other sign. The Libra third house is not particularly aggressive about expressing its own ideas.

It is only through the Aries ninth that this person can experience himself. He seeks one-mindedness and a conclusive singular viewpoint to all the ideas that are presented to him. The desire to be one with another and the desire to be one alone cannot always be achieved at the same time. On a sexual level, this presents a peculiar kind of paradox. The Venus rulership of the Libra third house symbolizes the seeking of love through relationships. At the same time, the Mars rulership of the Aries ninth house shows that a sexual consciousness is best maintained by not allowing the self to become one with another. Too much blending reduces sexual attraction. The desire to not blend with another, while encreasing sexual attraction, may prevent the achievement of a love consciousness.

The lesson of this polarity is in learning how to balance sexual attitudes with the very basic need for love. When the lower mind finds harmony between the self and another, then the higher mind can begin to understand the one-mindedness that is possible through a well-balanced relationship.

KEYWORDS: gentle, peacemaker, sometimes sexually defensive, seeks to balance expression, creative, more sensual than sexual, strength sometimes blocked by passive nature, needs freedom within a relationship, sexual experiences build the higher self, contrary thoughts, sexual competition presents conflict, childlike qualities, youthful attitudes, relationships balance the ego.

Scorpio Third House— Taurus Ninth House

With this placement nearly all communication is sexual. The individual is extremely telepathic and knows how to reach another through unconscious levels. He is highly sensitive to the undertones of language. If Virgo in the first house accompanies this placement, then some of the extreme intensity is leveled off. This person is always thinking sexually and is aware of it. He mentally undresses people while appearing to remain the outward paragon of virtue. He will bring others to the subject of sex by reading their aura in order to focus on any sexual thoughts they carry. Thus, he is capable of turning non-sexual situations into sexual ones, but always making it look like the responsibility falls on the other person.

Once sex has become physical, his art of deep intense communication takes on a very different role. If he feels accepted, then he likes to be quite expressive during the sexual act. He often has a "bedroom voice" to begin with, and once he lets go, there is no limit to the ways he can arouse his partner. For some people, he seems to be too much, for his communicative ability goes deeper than sex itself. Through the act he begins making his partner aware of subconscious thought entities that were locked below the individual's threshold of awareness; and because of this he has a way of showing his lover a part of herself that might otherwise take psychiatrists years to uncover. Much of this occurs because he has an insistent quality that likes to go right to the core of things.

The Taurus ninth house adds a persistant quality to the sexual consciousness. Since this polarity is fixed, there is tenacity in attached to the thought processes. The Taurean harmony of the higher mind tries to cling to its comfortable place in nature. The turbulence of Scorpio emotions come out in relationships and keeps creating transformations that the Taurean attitude tries to resist. The qualities of consistency, devotion, sincerity and loyalty are demanded of a partner.

This is a highly sexual placement for the third and ninth house polarity. The superficial quality of the third house becomes extremely deep due to the Scorpio rulership. Sexual thought is pushed to action as the higher mind needs physical touching in order to communicate.

The lesson inherent in this placement is to accept one's sexuality, without trying to make it less for the sake of acceptance by another. If the individual denies his sexuality, he seems to lose touch with himself. If he realizes his needs, he may offend others who resent his frankness, but he will feel more centered. Even when he sees himself sabotaging relationships because of the Scorpio third house, he must know it is for a reason his higher mind demands.

KEYWORDS: vital need for self-expression, deep thinker, sensitive to partner's unconscious thoughts, intuitive, lustful, powerful, thoughts, code-breaker, psychic tendencies, unconscious jealousies hurt relationships, incestuous thoughts, possessive thoughts, unpretentious, seeks fullness, possible bi-sexual feelings, intense, strong, can be obsessed with power.

Sagittarius Third House— Gemini Ninth House

This is a difficult house polarity which often manifests itself as a lack of perspective regarding the true nature of relationships between things and people. The individual tends to place too much emphasis on trivial thoughts while neglecting major issues. He can find answers to problems, but somehow he never finds a solution! He repeatedly mulls over situations, seeking correctness rather than answers. He may be too philosophical about intimate personal matters. He may try to personalize impersonal philosophical ideals.

On a sexual level he may be one of the most frustrated individuals in the entire zodiac for he seldom believes he has conveyed all of his ideas to his partner. In the act itself, he may be mentally preoccupied. Many with this placement have Taurus in the eighth house. When these two signs combine, there is a tendency to become sexually jaded at an early age through oversatiation.

The Gemini-Sagittarius polarity carries inner fears of being trapped by situations that might become too confining. There is a desire to be pursued but not caught! The individual tries to find relationships without the tight boundaries that might make him mentally stagnant.

When the Gemini ninth house is used correctly, it can help the individual eventually understand his relationships. Neither of the signs in this polarity are particularly fixated on sexuality. Instead, there is a focus of attention on mental understanding. Curiosity rates higher than actual sexual activity. It's important, to find a relationship based on truth and understanding. A partner helps balance exaggerated thoughts that come from an over-idealistic perception of reality. When the individual realizes that he is paying too much attention to trivia and not enough to main issues, he can begin to understand all that another person has to offer him.

KEYWORDS: abundant ideas, talkative, scatters mental energies, popular, philosophical relationships, sexually frustrated, needs freedom in relationships, often difficulty reaching orgasm, dissipating, obsessive thoughts, exaggerated ideas, relationships with foreigners, mental roaming, needs practical and focused partner.

Capricorn Third House— Cancer Ninth House

With Capricorn in the third house, communication is centered around problem solving. It is not easy for the individual to express what he feels because he feels things too deeply. He may set up blocks between what he understands and what he thinks he should tell others.

In his sexual relationships it takes him a long time to open up because he must trust his partner before he can reveal his ideas, thoughts or true feelings. He either throws himself into meaningless relationships where self-revelation is unnecessary, or he waits a long time in order to develop the lasting stable relationship that he is truly seeking. When he is able to communicate, he can say more with less words than any sign in the zodiac, for he only focuses on something if it fulfills two criteria. First, the idea must be extremely purposeful, and second, it must have enough power behind it to last a long time. He needs to believe that he is in control sexually. He rarely picks partners unless they have some hidden potential. Each relationship becomes something of a project and he measures his success by how well the other individual responds to all the ideas he mystically transfers.

This placement makes the mind attracted to individuals who are growing, building or achieving new stature in their lives or contributing something to the society they live in.

The reserved thought processes of the Capricorn third house, are in harmony with the ninth house Cancerian desire to find a spiritual home. Truth is determined by how long truth lasts. Security is also measured this same way. He forms mental constructs through his Capricorn third house. With each new person he meets, he neatly fits them into one or another mind structure. By doing this, he measures their ultimate value in his life. When he can see ultimate value in another, he will do everything he can to nourish their consciousness.

Sex is something that must have meaning and purpose. It is seen as something which either brings out the deep meaning of future plans, or else as a worthless endeavor which can sidetrack one from the solidity of the present.

The lesson in this polarity is that emotions can only be raised to a spiritual level when they are expressed in relationships that have ultimate value. Thus, the idea of sexual vulnerability is only possible when true emotional security is felt on a spiritual level.

KEYWORDS: deeply sensitive, restricts expression, mystical, seeks deep meaning through relationships, great wisdom, learns through experience, seeks deep understanding, secretive, closed when threatened, can only be reached through spiritual love, conservative ideas, patient, protective, defensive, highly selective.

Aquarius Third House— Leo Ninth House

With Aquarius in the third house, sexual communication takes many forms. The individual is extremely curious. He also fears deep commitments, preferring to keep himself somewhat free should something new and better present itself. When this third house is accompanied by Sagittarius in the first, marriage may be avoided due to the roaming and wandering tendencies of the combination of these two signs.

On a sexual level, this person tries to live out his ideas of freedom which may not be generally accepted by current standards. Sometimes he is interested in bisexual or platonic relationships, seeking to understand what he has not yet experienced. He is highly sensitive to thought currents, particularly those which represent progressive ideas. He is a "firster," finding the first-time experiences hold more meaning for him than repeating the same experiences with the same people. His strongest sensitivities are awakened when he sees himself in sexual situations that he never imagined he could cope with, and yet secretly wished would present themselves. This is the one position in the zodiac where "three or more" might not necessarily be a crowd!

With the combined influence of the Sun and Jupiter ruling the Leo ninth house, the need for mental freedom is enhanced. Limiting situations are usually thrown off as being detrimental to the needs of the self. The Aquarius-Leo polarity is extremely creative, and needs room, breadth, and scope to expand so the individual can feel in tune with the universe.

On lower mind levels he can appear aloof when in fact he is really very caring.

Sex is part of the exploration of life. It is a path of discovery through which new dimensions can be reached. The lesson of this polarity is to blend the Aquarius-Leo qualities of discovery with personal value. When his thoughts are focused toward all that is new and different, he can contribute to his society and on a personal level to those he loves, providing he doesn't lose sight of the fact that his thoughts and ideas represent his seeds for creation. The lower mind must become more responsible, so he can confront the higher mind of Leo, which cannot shirk facing itself.

KEYWORDS: unconventional ideas, stimulating, unusual estrangements, creates bedlam, curious, free-thinking, future-oriented, independent, kinky, mentally agile, original, versatile, adaptable, misunderstood, loner, irresponsible relationships, difficulty in marriage, stubborn, strong mind, powerful will, excitement-oriented, experimental, voyeuristic, secretly-principled, bizarre relationships, mentally aggressive.

Pisces Third House—
Virgo Ninth House

With Pisces in the third house, the individual seeks wispy dreamlike relationships. Every fiber of his being can be sexually sensitive. He is particularly drawn by people's eyes, for he can feel their entire essence through them. He communicates by creating powerful romantic illusions that few (often even himself) can see through.

His relationships are vague, for he does not like boundaries. He tries to draw people into himself through his words and is often successful. In non-verbal ways, the sex act represents an opportunity for him to communicate his perception of a greater cosmic reality. The Neptunian quality of this placement enables the individual to teach his partners how to swim through time and space to a better understanding of who they really are. Therefore, it is not the vague impressions of language and thought that make this placement special, but rather the silent ways in which it puts an individual in touch with infinite understanding. When love comes from the infinite, it is soft and gentle, soothing and mellow. Relationships take on unique and mystical character. A mystifying and haunting quality in the personality lures others to the great depths of understanding that this indivudal sees as merely his natural way of being.

The Virgo ninth house, however, makes it difficult for the individual to see his own essence. The mind may seek a small-minded view of perfection when in fact it is capable of knowing things that are truly beyond the finite conception of what is perfect. The higher mind tends to judge the lower mind, attempting to make it fit rigid standards.

The fear of missing something causes him to focus on too many details. This can be a blessing and a curse—for much that he sees disappoints him. On very deep levels he truly loves people, for his higher mind is dedicated to the humane. He is afraid that others may make him vulnerable. He may feel that the purest part of him, is private. He realizes that the best way for others to invade this private part of himself is through his sexuality. As a result, his sexual behavior patterns are usually defensive.

What he often fails to realize is that his Pisces third house effortlessly knows all that his Virgo ninth house is trying to discover. He can achieve harmony with himself by realizing the cosmic awarness that he experiences when relating to others is truly a product of the ideals that his higher mind has known all the time. The lesson of this polarity is for the individual to overcome his tendency to judge the sexual nuances of relationships which actually put him in touch with his Divine nature. Analyzing the reasons why he thinks the way he does only serves to lower his consciousness by deluding him into thinking that he can control the subtle force that is moving his consciousness. In this very special placement, the Neptune-ruled third house shows the clearness of universal thought while the Mercury-ruled ninth actually is the illusion!

KEYWORDS: misunderstood, sensitive, intuitive, misadventures, slippery, evasive, analyzes impressions, magnetic, mystifying, intriguing, sexually haunting, mistrusts own thoughts, idealistic, judgemental of partner's values, hypnotic, watchful, nebulous with a reason, difficulty understanding impressions, idealistic.

8. The Fourth and Tenth Houses

The fourth house symbolizes our roots. It is the foundation upon which the rest of the chart is built. From parental teachings and the experiences of the early childhood years our instinctual patterns are formed. Regardless of where we are or the company we keep we will act out the different roles we learned during these formative years.

The fourth house symbolizes the womb that we carry around ourselves as a protection from external circumstances. Sexual partners may become surrogate mothers, fathers, aunts, uncles, etc., as we keep reestablishing the foundations which once represented comfort and safety. The more others are able to fulfill memories of childhood roles, the more we are able to respond to them and retain the child within.

As the core of emotions, this house governs the way we react to the circumstances of life. In essence, it symbolizes the way we feel on an instinctual level. When we stray outside this framework, we feel threatened and want to earn our way back (in effect to the proverbial womb). As the foundation of all of our instinctual emotional patterns, the fourth house symbolizes the patterns of life we are comfortable with.

This house symbolizes the roots of the Oedipus complex that we must work through in order to become adults. In mythology, Oedipus Rex (born the son of a king and a queen) was raised by people who were not his parents. One day, as he was approaching manhood, an oracle said "he would kill his father and marry his mother." This idea was so repulsive to Oedipus that he decided to leave home in order to make the prediction false. On the road he met a stranger who would not let him pass. They got into a heated argument and Oedipus slew the stranger on his way. Finally he arrived at a distant kingdom and fell in love with a widowed queen. Later he discovered that the queen was his real mother, and the man he slew on the road was his real father. Oedipus ran away, because he could not cope with this knowledge.

Sigmund Freud began to research the implications of the myth. He discovered that young male children become quite jealous when they see the father approaching the mother with any feelings of love, and they begin to view the father as a competitor. Freud drew the conclusion that every male child (looking at it in a very simplistic way) loves his mother and sees the father as a threat to the mother/son relationship. This occurs in reverse for the female child. The love she feels for her father is coupled with feelings of competition toward her mother. Freud called this the Electra complex. There is no doubt that to some extent the Oedipus-Electra complex plays a role in our emotional beginnings. Most individuals outgrow these feelings while some carry them throughout life, constantly seeking substitute people through whom they can re-enact the same childhood feelings and traumas. There is no better place to act out such feelings than in a sexual situation. The person may choose to replay the child (but now with adult strength and virility), viewing the sexual partner as the parental figure who was denied them in youth. Adult reactions to rival lovers shows this clearly. Oedipal lingering may be present when people are sexually attracted to those many years younger or older than they are.

All these feelings and the subtle twists they take through life come from the fourth house. The memories stored in the fourth house become the emotional chronology of an individual's sexual history. The seeds of these memories ultimately become the building blocks that will form the structure of adult life through the tenth house. The tenth house symbolizes the domineering parent figure. In order to reach adulthood, this figure must be confronted, whether it be father, mother, or surrogate figures to whom the individual relates.

Through the tenth house, we seek meaning in life by building the qualities that have purpose. To become free of early age authority figures, the individual must develop a great deal of power within himself. The eventual goal is a state of adult sufficiency. Where the fourth house responds through dependency, the tenth house symbolizes the emerging self that has overcome the domineering ghosts of childhood. It is here that the individual strives to master all that had mastered him in the past.

On a sexual level there is a deeply hidden psychological meaning to the tenth house. Every individual has a goal or a purpose in life. These add meaning and substance to his existence. Often the desire to reach these goals comes from early childhood. Yet, because a child cannot live in an adult reality, the goals become hidden in fantasy. Year after year they are nurtured in the individual's imagination.

Saturn is the natural ruler of the tenth and Saturn is a container. Underneath its solid facade, all the dream fantasies and wishes that are as yet unrealized are creatively linked to the sex act itself (which from the inception of the very first thought of it to its completion in coitus) is the symbolic inspirational idealization of a goal, the striving towards it, and the ultimate achievement of it.

In this respect, Saturn must also be understood as the planet of patterns. People have sexual behavior patterns which they tend to keep repeating. Their fantasies are also patterned. The dreams, wishes, sexual stories, fantasies, etc., may seem to vary from one fantasy to another but there is always a common thread that runs through them. It is this common thread that gives the clue to what an individual has to overcome in his real life existence in order to reach the goals he truly wants.

The fourth and tenth house polarity is a chronological one. It starts in the growth patterns of childhood; it moves to the way in which "guided fantasies" ultimately manifest themselves in the creative reality of the individual's adult life.

Aries Fourth House— Libra Tenth House

With Aries in the fourth house, the emotional nature stays at immature levels long into adulthood. The driving desire here is to individualize the child within the self, thus separating the ego from the collective ego of family. One of the ways this can be achieved is by acting out challenges through which the individual can emerge emotionally victorious. Usually he overreacts, but it is the most natural way for him to convince himself that he actually is his own person.

He may be sexually attracted to individuals younger than himself. If he still carries unconscious childhood resentments at being denied any of his desires, he may have sadistic tendencies. By subjugating his partner, he symbolically becomes the emotional master. He may be aware that he is playing a game but he seldom knows how to control the temper tantrums his unconscious creates at each possibility of rejection. Herein lies his greatest fear, for his primitive emotional level always feels that it is fighting for its very existence. Through the Libra tenth house he wants harmony with his peer group and does not like to make waves. He may never really know what is right for him and what isn't. He may seesaw from one extreme to another. He has a powerful attraction to asthetics—poetry, art, music, crafts or hobbies are important throughout his life. He feels competitive which causes an imbalance, for a peaceful sense of security is his primary goal. He learns that the best way of achieving peace is through noninvolvement. By being interested, but noncommittal, he can literally walk between the drops in a rainstorm without getting wet.

He experiences both yin and yang feelings; he approaches and avoids his goals at the same time. Always considering both sides, he believes that taking any affirmative stand on one makes him automatically miss the other. Thus, he vascillates between an agressive emotionality and the sometimes passive way he actually tastes life.

On a sexual level there is usually an active fantasy life that he both does and does not want to actuate in reality. He wants to experience his fantasies but is sometimes afraid that they will control him. He is afraid of overdoing anything because he knows how easy it is for him to become too involved. In order to protect himself from himself his sexual fantasies are usually incomplete. He never goes beyone the point where he will lose control of the passive nature he is seeking. His career goals are the same for he is afraid of wanting too much and unsatisfied with too little. His desire is to find the balance that makes him experience "normalcy." He has sexual fantasies that are deviant from the norm and he is afraid they will not be accepted by his partner. In both career and sex, he needs the encouragement and prodding of others in order to realize his secret desires. He must learn that he can maintain balance and harmony without having to hide himself inside himself.

The emotional thrust of the Aries fourth house is always pushing toward new beginnings that must be balanced through the Libra tenth house. Childhood sexual impulses must ultimately mature into a balanced understanding of love before the individual can be happy.

The lesson of this placement is to be able to take narcissistic sexual fantasies from childhood and to convert them into a powerful sense of soul identity so that the substance which is necessary in order to share with another is formed.*

KEYWORDS: vibrant soul, emotionally independent, much hidden sexuality, eager, hidden aggression, incestual feelings, primitive ego, hidden need to dominate, masturbatory, pacifies authority figures, must balance compulsive instincts.

Taurus Fourth House— Scorpio Tenth House

With this placement, the individual responds to sexuality that offers security. He needs to be held and reassured and as this sense of personal safety is confirmed he will give of himself. The most important thing in his life is to feel a firm foundation beneath him. He doesn't like to take chances and is slow to trust new people in his life. This person roots the emotions very strongly in material reality. He builds his security by seeking lovers that represent financial gain or prestige. He is unconsciously trying to resist facing childhood complexes and usually does not resolve them until after mid-life. In order to preserve the memories of his early years, he seeks partners who have something in common with the parent of the opposite sex.

---

*The Libra tenth house is more similar to retrograde Venus in the tenth house. See Martin Schulman, *Karmic Astrology, Vol. 2, Retrogrades and Reincarnation* (York Beach, ME: Samuel Weiser, 1978): 18-19.

This assures him of an unconscious continuity within whose framework he feels protected.

Basically, he is emotionally shy and needs a strong partner as indicated by the fact that this chart placement is often accompanied by Leo in the seventh house. From the partner, he develops his ego strength. In return, he will have to supply a strong emotional foundation upon which a powerful union can be built.

Mystically, this placement is called the "mother of illumination," for through its slow methodical maturing process it ultimately brings to fruition the enlightenment of the emotional self. Dreams and fantasies are strongly linked to reality. They are nutured under the protective covering of the earth, and somehow through some circumstance or other, the volatile intensity of the Scorpio tenth house causes them to erupt into a series of events and changes which bring about complete transformation in the individual's being.

As an adult, this person is complacent but never satisfied. The Scorpio intensity makes him highly conscious of how others reach for their goals. He can be jealous of others if he does not see more progress in his life than he sees in theirs.

He is secretive for he feels that by keeping his motives to himself he eventually can spring the trap that will open doors to the success he seeks. There may be a great deal of unconscious paranoia with this placement as he feels that others are somehow capable of stealing his "place in the sun." He tries to push himself ahead of his peers as if to overcome his fear of being left behind.

He sees the unconscious weaknesses of any competitor. In this way he tries to insure his chances for success.

On a sexual level, nearly all his fantasies involve something which is destructive to the other person. He tries to make his partner reveal herself while he stays safely behind his wall, fully protected as he disarms his sexual partner. On a more gross level he may lean toward sadistically de-sexing his partners. This makes him feel that he has eliminated competition. There may be an unconscious cruelty syndrome accompanying this placement.

It should be remembered that Scorpio is a ruthless sign on an unconscious level and, when one considers this sign in terms of goals or achievements, there is little that this individual would not do—no matter how much it may harm or hurt another. This is a powerful placement carrying with it a potent lesson to be learned. If one uses power to take advantage of others when they are weak, then one must constantly guard against the day when those individuals grow strong. When sexual magnetisum is used to secure power, it can only lead to unhappy conditions. When this individual learns to blend his sexuality with his giving Taurean love nature, then all he experiences in life will be greatly enriched.

KEYWORDS: Powerful sexual feelings, sexual attractions at work, shy childhood, need to dominate, creates sexual challenges, alluring, slow-maturing, builds ego strength from others, stubborn emotions, extremely sensitive, overpowering.

Gemini Fourth House— Sagittarus Tenth House

With Gemini in the fourth house, the emotional self is strongly linked with the individual's mental outlook. At the very core of his foundation is an abundance of unresolved ideas. His emotional attraction to the opposite sex is based on his need to explore those ideas. Much of his sexuality is mental. Sometimes this placement indicates a broken home in early childhood. When this is not the case, it shows an identity problem stemming from the family relationship. Dual standards in the emotional make-up may not be recognized until mid-life. The individual may spend a great deal of energy running away from self-confrontations. He needs sex partners who will help him organize his thoughts, teach him how to understand yin and yang emotional patterns, and help him to confront his unconscious duality.

In physical sex he is a student of relationship-interplay, often hiding himself so he can watch the scenario unfold. His development may linger beyond his chronological age. This can manifest as those sexual attractions that remind him of things that aroused his sexual interest during his elementary school years. There are few signs as emotionally insecure as the Gemini fourth house, for at the very roots of his soul he finds himself leading a double life. His changing philosophical goals are difficult to define. He must make the journey through his Sagittarius tenth house in order to find what life has for him. He wants to travel. He wants to be honored, receive medals, trophies and awards. He wants the freedom to change his goals as often as the mood strikes him. Life becomes a series of journeys rather than ever feeling settled in one place. He fantasizes what it would be like to roam, to drift, to be a romantic, a person of the world, to understand many languages, to know the customs of different countries, philosophies, or religions. Basically he imagines feeling at home wherever he might want to go.

On his sexual level, he imagines women who are of a different religion, philosophy or culture. His mind roams from one person to another, wanting to experience the broad spectrum of all that each new individual has to offer. He has difficulty centering himself for his life often revolves around the individuals he tries to experience. Because he wants to know about so many things, so many people, so many places, he may be far less centered than any of the people he knows.

He tends to avoid situations and relationships in which he could become intimately vulnerable. By remaining noncommittal he is able to maintain the sense of freedom that allows him to continue his wandering imagination. There is strong discontent with the here and "Now."* If he could only heed the words of the Don MacLean song, "all roads lead to where I stand," he would reach contentment.

The sexual nature of any chart with this placement is not so much based on physical experiences as it is the consciousness of the individual. The signs Gemini and Sagittarus have to do with mutations that take place in the mind. The actual journey through life and even the physical experiences of sex are only the outer manifestations of how the individual's mind is constantly changing its journey within itself. The lesson of this placement is for the mind to understand itself through all its travels.

KEYWORDS: emotional duality, sometimes bisexual, sexually curious, experimental, repetitive experiences, flirtatious, noncommittal, wanderlust, inconstant, risk instinct, freedom loving, emotionally undependable partner, needs psychic space, analytic emotions, catalyst to others, unconscioulsy insecure, must resolve cleavages within the soul.

---

*See Martin Schulman, *Karmic Astrology, Vol. 4, The Karma of the Now* (York Beach, ME: Samuel Weiser, 1978).

Cancer Fourth House— Capricorn Tenth House

Cancer is in its rulership when it appears in the fourth house. Here it affords the individual the full gamut of emotions that he needs in order to richly experience all that life has to offer. Because this sign rules the home and one's environment, the individual's sexual interest is affected by the setting, tone and mood of his surroundings. Soft music, romantic candlelight, or a cozy atmosphere makes him particularly responsive to sexual provocation. He must also feel that his partner is offering future security. It is the enduring emotional stability of sex with one partner that allows him to be vulnerable enough to experience the richness he seeks. Without the promise of this, he unconsciously feels threatened; for too many encounters threaten his sense of stability. Where the promise of emotional security is present, however, he is extremely warm and giving in all ways.

Through the Capricorn tenth house this individual can experience a healthy structure of goals and the knowledge of how to work toward fulfilling them. Unlike so many other positions in the zodiac, he never says to himself "I would like to do this," or "I would like to achieve that." He does without talking about doing. He achieves without dreaming about achieving. He becomes fulfilled because he understands the structure of fulfillment.

His strongest characteristic is his ability to put shelves in his mind so that everything has its proper place. More than any other sign in the zodiac, he knows the secret of reaching goals. First he envisions the goal in its end result. Then if it is truly what he wants and if he believes he is capable of reaching it, he starts retracing his steps backward to the beginning of the inspiration. Then slow and plodding, he takes one step at a time in the direction of the goal. This achievement-oriented pattern begins early in childhood for he gives much thought to what is expected of him. At times he tries to escape by making his childhood linger on, long after he has truly outgrown it. But once he is ready to make his mark, he has very little interest in fantasy life. Knowing the difference between dreams and reality, he only fantasizes about what he can make a reality.

He has a keen interest in sexuality which is directly related to all his other goals in life. He is attracted to situations that are possible and practical and learns how to quickly dismiss those situations which would dissipate energy. The expression of sexuality must fit into what his family, ancestors, or his peer group expect of him. The lesson in this placement is for the individual to integrate his sexuality with his needs and feelings so the different facets of life can come together into a harmonious blend which will ultimately become his security.

KEYWORDS: seeks relationship continuity, needs deep meaning, strong attachments, fears loneliness, security conscious, reserved sexual emotions, seeks sexual dignity, protective, responsible, family conscious, struggle for self-identity through marriage, constant, needs sincerity.

Leo Fourth House— Aquarius Tenth House

This placement is built on creative power. The individual responds best to sexual situations in which he has the opportunity to display his command of himself along with his creative imagination as a unique and generous lover.

Usually he comes from a childhood where he experienced some oppression by at least one domineering parent. The effect is visible in his adult approach to sexuality. On an unconscious level he tries to overcome the parent who was an obstacle to him as a child. As a result, he is usually attracted to members of the opposite sex who represent a strong emotional challenge for him to overcome. He tends to attract powerful people who keep recreating the stimulus of power that he felt in youth. Lovers guide him toward achievement, and sex becomes a symbolic catalyst. Sometimes there are exhibitionist tendencies in an attempt to seek appreciation and approval.

As a child, there are usually difficulties because he has a tendency to think ahead of his classmates, age level, time in history, etc. His parents may try to mold him. As the promise of his Aquarius tenth house is luring him into the future, his powerful will makes him a "rule-breaker" in every possible area. He does this not for spite, which is often the way it is interpreted by others, or even to be contrary, but in order to keep himself from getting bogged down in what is already established. If he allows himself to follow established patterns of others, he will never achieve his own unique goal of trend setting.

On a sexual level, his early childhood fantasies are of an experimental nature. His sex drive tends to be somewhat unique. The common thread that runs through all of his fantasies is his insatiable curiosity. He can experiment with sexual situations that others would hardly even imagine but, the more bizarre and different they are, the more they stimulate his imagination in other areas by bringing out his creative power. He is able to begin replacing each fantasy with a bounty of new ideas.

The lesson of this placement revolves around the creative use of power for the benefit of humanity. On a sexual level, this means leading with kindness, guiding with humility, and teaching another to experience the power of creative love.

KEYWORDS: strong sexual needs, exhibitionist tendencies, generous with affections, must overcome domineering parent, power conscious, fear of being dominated, willful, versatile, attention seeking, powerful ego, unconscious overconcern with sexual performance.

Virgo Fourth House— Pisces Tenth House

With Virgo in the fourth house, the emotional nature is often stifled by narrow boundaries that do not give the individual freedom to expand. He may attempt to keep his emotions confined within boundaries which set limits to his experience. Or he tries to expand his emotions by analyzing them—a method which really doesn't work at all. He believes that if he can understand what makes him tick, he can function better. Functioning is not the key to sexuality, however, for it doesn't give a person the feeling of fulfillment. Fulfillment comes from allowing one's feelings to flow.

Many different types of psychological blocks affecting sexual expression may occur, running the gamut from difficulty experiencing orgasm, extended periods of frigidity or celibacy, bisexual desires, analytically avoiding intimate contact with the "base" qualities of sex. The individual may be unconsciously motivated to live up to the image of parental authority. During the childhood years he may have absorbed logical but subliminal ideas of God's expectations. These images may be transferred to a surrogate parent figure in the outside world as the individual consciously tries to emerge from his rigid unconscious emotional structure.

The Pisces tenth house adds a tinge of unreality to the Virgoan stiffness. Boxed in by a world of structure that does not allow the full self to be experienced, the individual may develop an active fantasy life. In essence he lives in a dream. He may stay as a child long into his adult life, not wanting to recognize the responsibilities that he feels. Whether he seeks to become a musician, artist, missionary, nurse or any other endeavor, his goals are influenced by his compassion for mankind.

Although his great compassion for others may start early in childhood, his own cupboard is not yet filled. He may find imaginative fantasies to replace his need for compassion. He may begin to invent sexual fantasies in which he unconsciously is serving the needs of another. As these fantasies develop, he may become interested in masochistic activities in an effort to help build another person's ego. He may have fantasies about putting himself down in some sexual way. He may be attracted to pictures or films which are "observer replacements" for his sex drive. When he is creative, he likes to observe his own creations. He may be in touch with the pure essence of creative reality if he knows how to use the dream state constructively. Few people can understand his reasoning or the methods he uses to achieve his goals. If he is highly evolved, and other chart indicators cooperate with this placement, he can function much like an Edgar Cayce, constantly helping others understand the finer music that exists.

In all his sexual fantasies he is more sensual than sexual. He is more romantic and imaginative than he is crude; he seeks gentle, loving outlets rather than coarse or base sexual experiences for they shake him too much out of his dream state. During the periods in life when he is not really achieving much in a career sense, his sexual expression may be voyeuristic as he goes through an observing phase. This changes as he directs his energies more actively toward what he really wants; and interesting enough, what he wants is usually for another rather than himself. As a result, his career goal drive often has to be stimulated by others for he is not the strongest self-starter.

The lesson of this placement is to build a creative reality by merging the infinite qualities of the dream state within the framework of the finite boundaries of practical reason. Once the lower emotions of the fourth house are purified through Virgo, the individual can begin to taste the higher forms of Divine Love.

KEYWORDS: emotional rigidity, sexual avoidance in childhood, difficulty with emotional surrender during physical sexuality, secretly judgemental of sex, fear of authority figures, timid, shy, hypersensitive, desires perfection, emotionally idealistic, clairvoyant, tests others, extremely giving soul, visionary, altruistic, self-critical, capable of Divine Love.

Libra Fourth House— Aries Tenth House

The individual experiences an obscure emotional struggle finding out who he is. He cannot decide whether the male or female parent deserves priority. He may swing like a pendulum between unconscious male and female identification. This causes so much inner confusion that he tends to lose his sense of being grounded by trying to run away from any sexual emotions that contradict themselves. In order to establish an inner grounding mechanism, he tends to attach himself to people who offer the appearance of being a firm foundation. On a sexual level, he has a tendency to choose partners who seem very sure of their own sexual identification. From these partners he tries to center himself by identifying with the root of their emotional strength.

His biggest problem is his feelings; experiencing the sureness it takes to act on them. He senses an "aloneness" that never quite allows him to feel sure that he really belongs to someone. This belonging to someone is his strongest emotional need. He will go out of his way, perhaps sacrificing his own inner harmony, in order to be part of another person's reality. By doing this he establishes a feeling of acceptance.

His sexual emotions get redirected through his career. The fear of rejection is so strong that he must literally force himself to be first or best in order to be sure that he will not be excluded from the center of things. In order to learn how to do this, the sexual fantasy level created in childhood is always centered around the overcoming of obstacles. As the person grows up, many of the details of these early fantasies may be covered as the Saturn ruled tenth house builds new structured patterns over the old ones. The person may become adept at mental sexual-suggestion for he can test his power at conquering the will of another. His fantasies have a hidden narcissistic tinge along with a constant sense of trying. He is attracted to that which he has to try to conquer. If there is nothing to conquer he is not really interested. This applies to both sexual expression and career direction. His most hidden sexual desires always involve trying something that he feels he doesn't know how to do or about which he is unsure. What he achieves in life (or what he gets out of sex) is not so much the finish as it is the joy of trying.

The balance between self-surrender and self-assertion is the keynote of the Libra-Aries polarity. The lesson here is that the self can be built unselfishly when sexuality is expressed with love.

KEYWORDS: youthful, not grounded, unsure of male-female sexual identification, need for emotional fairness, non-committal to others, strong need for acceptance, discouraging childhood, cannot handle rejection, develops strength through setbacks, sometimes narcissistic, spontaneous attractions, loneliness, needs mate with strong values.

Scorpio Fourth House— Taurus Tenth House

With this placement the emotional level is based on a shaky underpinning. There is constant turmoil and upheaval at the very roots of the soul which makes the individual try to regenerate his feelings about himself. He is seeking to control the seeds of destruction that he feels within, for they are ceaselessly gnawing away at any sense of solidarity and security he establishes. Sometimes this position shows a broken home at an early age. In less extreme cases the person feels that the rug will be pulled out from under himself at any moment. For this reason many people with a Scorpio fourth house go through promiscuous phases in life. They feel they have little to lose and everything to gain by reaching out for any form of love that can warm them. Their need is very great, yet no matter how much they experience, they seem to have a thirst that is unquenchable.

The real need can manifest through striving to obtain things that bring comfort to the senses. The individual wants to assure himself of his security. He tends to overdo, overwant, or to believe that he needs more than he does. He must some day be able to possess a lot of money or the power that it can give him, so any time his security is threatened he can somehow buy it back. This individual is only sure of what he owns, and what he owns should be in sight all the time! Because of the lack of stability in his early childhood, his outlook on life is unsure. He always has the feeling that somehow his life will fall apart beneath his feet. He thinks that if he can exert control over all the factors and people in his life he can buffer himself from experiencing this feeling or dealing with the fears that it arouses in him.

The childhood sexual fantasies are often lustful and self-destructive; but if one looks at the pattern they form, there is always an aim at securing, holding, firming, even imprisoning the partner, so that the individual wil not lose what he wants. He wants to be sexually dominant to the point of owning the other person. There are tendencies toward paranoia which can be alleviated if he reaches a real life goal in which he is in a socially acceptable power position. The turbulent emotional transformations that are constantly occurring cause him to become infuriated at the slightest rejection. Sometimes he feels almost as if he is falling off the earth into some deep, dark dungeon of imagined unconscious monsters. He needs a sexually submissive and slightly masochistic partner who will nevertheless encourage him to achieve the career stability and power that will ultimately give him the security he is crying out for.

The lesson of this placement is to allow all the emotions of sexual upheaval to transform themselves into creative love. This is accomplished only through the process of surrendering to the Higher Self.

KEYWORDS: emotional, upheaval, lustful, sometimes promiscuous, intense search for secure ground, misunderstood, constantly transforming emotional patterns, self-destructive, emotional battle at the roots of the soul, must rebuild past, capable of creative love, destructive relationships, experiences rejection, heavy karma during early years.*

Sagittarius Fourth House—
Gemini Tenth House

The Sagittarius fourth house indicates an emotional level that is consistantly in a state of flux. The individual is forever running towards new horizons or experiences that hold the vague promise of something better than what he feels. It is difficult for him to stay in the here and now for the grass always looks greener somewhere else. On a sexual level, he yearns for what he has not tasted. He may seek an unrealized ideal but never finds it. Instead, it is the emotional quest that ultimately becomes more important than the discovery of the ideal itself. He seeks freedom, and although he may say he wants security, he will purposely pick sex partners that encourage feelings of wanderlust.

In many ways he is an emotional nomad; moving from one feeling to another, one location to another or one relationship to another, finding each situation and circumstance lacking the fulfillment he knows is possible. In some cases, this placement leads to promiscuity because the seat of the emotions knows no limits or boundaries. Childhood fantasy is usually of a Don Quixote nature and the individual sees himself as a gallant adventurer. His swashbuckling emotions are usually very much out of proportion to the events and circumstances that trigger them.

In the younger years a kind of emotional wildness seems to pervade the entire being. Through the Gemini tenth house, maturity brings reason. The need to gain social acceptability forces this individual to communicate his thoughts and ideas on a more sound

---

*Martin Schulman, *Karmic Astrology, Vol. 1, The Moon's Nodes and Reincarnation* (York Beach, ME: Samuel Weiser, 1975): 29-32.

and realistic level. It is important that his words and thoughts are meaningful to others, for this assures him that that he is mentally worthwhile. Herein lies his greatest insecurity, for in truth he is not really sure of his mentality at all. During the childhood years, scattered interests take him in many directions at the same time. His youthful goals are unrealistic, not tied together and have no apparent connections with each other. As these goals become replaced by sexual fantasy, the child is able to temporarily relieve his frustrations through his imagination. The sexual patterns, however, tend to be scattered or involving many people, situations, and places, leaving the individual unsettled. When he grows up, he may not accept the incongruous nature of his thoughts. Instead of accepting the fact that he has scattered himself quite literally at the seams, it is much easier for him to see each desire as stemming from a different person. Thus, he starts to really need people, because through them, he can act out all the different drives in himself. It is difficult for a person with this house placement to be true to one person, for at his very core is a basically restless nature.

The individual can step outside of himself and not even know that he is doing it. He may do this often in order to see what he looks like from the view point of another. Often there are unconscious sexual fantasies of a voyeuristic nature, as the individual wants to vicariously view through others what he really wants to participate in himself but might not be brazen enough or honest enough with himself to admit. Underneath all the sham he would really like to experience sex with more than one person at a time or attend an orgy. Some people with this placement do. Others do it vicariously through reading pornographic literature. It doesn't matter. What does matter is that the individual is spending much of his life seeing his drives and goals in others rather than in himself.

The lesson here is that the ability to relate to others is founded upon how truthful and honest one can be with oneself.

KEYWORDS: expansive, exaggerates emotions, lacks discipline, relationships cause identity crisis, frivolous, seeks emotional freedom, lacks purpose, sometimes promiscuous, wild, free thinking, hurried, inconstant, versatile, adaptable, basic need for change, must learn emotional honesty.

Capricorn Fourth House—
Cancer Tenth House

The sign Capricorn is difficult in the fourth house since it is opposing its natural ruling position. Emotions become locked up or suppressed as the individual keeps trying to live up to the expectations of others. He strives to achieve and maintain the respect of elders (a feeling which was deeply ingrained during childhood). On a sexual level, this sometimes has the reverse effect of what one might expect. Instead of leading the individual to sexual behavior patterns that increase his sense of respectability, it sometimes causes hidden sexually irresponsible behavior. If the individual does not have to face his true emotions, than he can do whatever he wants in his sexual role. Usually he is avoiding confrontation with strong Oedipal problems which center around his having to be more grown up than he wanted to be during his childhood. When he chronologically reaches adulthood, a rebellious nature sets in and the baser sexual qualities of Capricorn begin to emerge. He can be extremely lustful until he feels he has an established foundation beneath him. Often this comes much later in life or after he has had a chance to sample the ways of the world and learn for himself.

Through the Cancer tenth house, the process of replacement has a tendency to become inverted. The fully grown child, old for his age in his youth, refuses to grow up when he is chronologically an adult. During his younger years, he establishes adult goals. He eventually replaces these goals in his sexual fantasy. His fantasy pattern is often fixated on adult figures doing adult things. This may be the child who dresses up in his or her parents' clothing, taking on the dominant adult role from an early age. However, when he reaches adulthood, there are strong feelings of missing the childhood—the childhood that was never truly experienced. Because of this, the person reaches, attempting to feel all the things other children did.

This is a rather unique behavorial characteristic, because it means that the individual fantasizes himself being a child when he is an adult. In this respect, a child is not to be held truly responsible for his actions. With this complex pattern, the person can not only feel that he truly does not have to meet adult goals but he can also fantasize and act out all the childlike sexual games he wants without receiving more than parent-to-child punishment for wrong actions. Thus, his sexual life does not include a realization of sexual repercussions for wrong actions (i.e. actions that either hurt another individual or the self or violate the laws) as one would find in the normal healthy restraints practiced by a complete adult.

His sexual patterns may center around either getting away with something or infringing on someone elses family structure to find this place. In the career area, he tends to drift and wander until he masters this problem and stops dissipating his energy trying to make up for times gone by.

The lesson here is to accept emotional responsibility so that adult life represents a new birth of self along with a completely new understanding of family ties and values.

KEYWORDS: inhibitions, hidden emotion, guilt-ridden, lonely, wants to build own foundations, misplaces responsibility feelings, stubborn, clings to past, deeply sensitive, Oedipal feelings, age conscious, lustful, selfish tendencies, must learn to accept emotional responsibilities.

Aquarius Fourth House— Leo Tenth House

With this placement the emotional level is highly independent and erratic. From moment to moment the individual keeps changing his mind about what actually represents his security. He is constantly questioning things just beyond the realm of his current understanding. To do this, however, he needs emotional freedom. He also tries to seek out a mate who doesn't.

Sometimes this placement leads to different types of sexual deviation all stemming from a keen sense of emotional curiosity. Sexual behavior may follow no pattern at all. There may be a psychological complex that keeps prompting this individual to understand his uniqueness. He may even have an emotional obsession about being different along with a fear of becoming too rooted in anything that would keep him from exploring

untired emotions. More than anything he needs to understand that the aloneness he experiences will disappear once he accepts that in his uniqueness he is not really different from anyone else. This problem of trying to be different becomes even more difficult because of the high expectations the individual has of himself through his Leo tenth house. He must somehow prove that he is capable of overcoming whatever might keep him from being what he wants to be. There is an obsessive drive to achieve some powerful goals. Ambition here is surpassed by no other sign in the zodiac, for it is prompted by the combination of will and power.

As a child, the individual senses what he must eventually accomplish but also sees other people as obstacles in his path. By studying them he learns what they have and how they use it in order to make the world bend to meet their desires. He is constantly frustrated because he cannot yet exert his own power. Thus he turns to the process of replacement.

He begins to invent sexual fantasies that put him in a powerful position. In these fantasies he creates scenarios which emphasize his unique sense of self-importance. As his sexual fantasies mature, his need for power takes on specific patterns. This individual can focus attention on the size of someones sex organs (as the unconscious roots of one's fantasy life always equate larger size to more power). He seeks members of the opposite sex who always seem unattainable. He likes battles for power during the sex act and tends to fall into the trap of being attracted to individuals because of a Venus or Adonis physical appearance rather than what they offer inside. The common thread that runs through his fantasies is that he is "the conqueror." And he doesn't stop here, for once he has conquered he must rule as well.

Instead of his fantasy patterns tapering off as he begins to achieve success in his career, they actually seem to increase. The idea of power lures him and, ironically, he is powerless to control this lure of power.

The lesson is to learn that the purpose of power is to gain command of the self. When this is accomplished, the unique experimental emotional qualities of the Aquarius fourth house can manifest in many creative areas that will bring the individual happiness.

KEYWORDS: willful, erratic emotional nature, futuristic, domineering tendencies, showy, curious, brazen, strong, colorful life, frightened by competition, possible homosexual or bisexual feelings, vivid imagination, seeks creative sexuality, powerful, leads relationships.

Pisces Fourth House— Virgo Tenth House

With this placement, the emotional level is strongly romantic. The individual never quite feels strong tangible foundations beneath him, but he does feel a constant calling to some distant music that seems to lull his soul into a hazy state of oblivion. He is in love with love and is able to see it where others cannot. It is difficult for him to hold on for the Neptunian nature of his emotions keeps alluding his grasp. He feels things, but he cannot put them in words. He knows things, but he cannot organize his thoughts. As a child, he learns to function completely on intuition and instinct rather than through reason and sensibility.

His highly passionate nature comes out when he is able to see a fine essence in a sex partner that he can relate to. He is extremely idealistic as well as gullible and he often finds himself believing what he wants to believe rather than what he intuitively knows. Every time he goes against his intuition, he is doing himself an injustice.

He may experience some sorrow in his early years which he keeps re-enacting in his sexuality. He finds relationships that throw him into masochistic roles until he is able to uncover the problem at its roots and dissolve it.

Through his Virgo tenth house, he sees the ideal of perfection and is afraid he will never be able to reach it. Criticism and rejection are extremely difficult to deal with because of basic insecurities.

During childhood he tries to replace the fear of rejection by a vivid imagination in which he envisions himself as some mythological, religious, spiritual or other figure that is in some way above the possibility of being rejected. On a sexual level, he must invent fantasies that are more related to service to oneself so that when he is old enough he can transfer these fantasies into actually being his own servant. Because of the nature of this replacement fantasy there is a strong tendency towards masturbation. Through this the individual learns how to accept himself, but as he grows older masturbation takes place on levels other than just sexual. Learning how to overcome timidity and find means of expressing the cosmic emotions that he feels actually becomes a life's work. Service to the self means coming out of oneself and feeling a sense of belonging in the world. There is a tendency to study emotions and be an observer of one's life. While there is much to be learned from this, strong feelings of loneliness accompany it. The individual must learn how to grow in the world rather than away from it. And, although all he sees is less idealistic than what he imagines, he must learn to accept not only the conditions that he sees around him but his own imperfections as well. On a sexual level, he is seeking union between the finite and the infinite.

The lesson is that the sensitivities in his creative emotions are part of the knowledge he is able to absorb from the universe in order to purify his goals. His deep sense of beauty along with his need for perfection can lead him to those experiences in life through which he will grow the most.

KEYWORDS: sensuous, must overcome emotional gullibility, dreamer, masochistic behavior, weak ego strength, cosmic emotion, passionate but inhibited, childlike tendencies, needs gentle mate, sympathetic, understanding, intuitive, compassionate nature, romantic, capable of saint-like characteristics, visionary, strong imagination, powerful beliefs, needs order to function.

9. The Fifth and Eleventh Houses

The fifth house rules the way an individual creates his life. Traditionally known as the house of love affairs, it describes what an individual tries to achieve through his sexual encounters. Every individual has flaws, idiosyncrasies, undeveloped potential and unrealized growth. Through this house, attempts are made to create more development by expressing the ideals and achievements that the individual feels are right for him.

Because this house is naturally under the influence of Leo, there is usually a desire to take command over the sexual partner in order to create the blossoming tree from all the undeveloped seeds the individual sees. If we don't feel our potential, the basic prerequisite for giving love is absent. Love is the ability to bring sunshine into the life of another or to create our ideal of love with our partner. This generally results in a molding effect. In the process of loving, we rub off on each other. There are people who leave a powerful and lasting effect on us because they show us our own abilities to create—abilities we may not have realized without this kind of love.

There are many forms of love and many ways of expressing it sexually. Some love appears to be not sexual at all, but on subliminal levels, even if the physical act is missing, it is. Where a physical sexual exchange takes place, the strongest molding effect takes place. An individual learns how to act in order to win the respect, admiration and adoration of another. And, depending upon how much he needs the other person, he will to different degrees either accept or reject this molding effect.

Under the natural rulership of the Sun the fifth house symbolizes the budding "child" in a person that can be brought to bloom. Creation develops through the unfoldment of patterns that grow out of each other. As a result, this house describes not so much the type of individual that one seeks as a lover, but rather the ideals of love one has. Through a love relationship the individual tries to find a partner who has the capacity of touching these ideals, and expressing them. This is the process of creation itself, for from one's ideal, come the creative efforts that one puts forth to build his reality. One of the most beautiful parables of Jesus speaks of a man who had a bag of seeds. He threw his seeds outward and some landed in sand and could not grow. Some landed on rocks and could not take root. Some landed in the path where men walked and were trampled. And, some landed in fertile soil and multiplied beyond expectation. Love is very much like this. The act of loving an individual is planting seeds and since loving is a choice that one makes through a conscious decision, then we have the choice of throwing our love indiscriminately to the wind, taking the chance that it will land in a worthy place, or purposefully planting our seeds of creation in the minds of fertile soil where each ounce of love will multiply and blossom. One cannot mold a rock, or give structure to sand. It would be fruitless to build anything on a path where careless feet would trod on gentle seeds. But, there is always fertile soil and love grows best under these conditions.

It is important to realize that you cannot love another without loving yourself first. In this respect it is difficult to love yourself without first feeling that there is a special niche or place in the universe where you belong. This can be understood through the eleventh house; unquestionably the most misunderstood house in astrology.

To understand this it is important to realize that astrology has two main purposes, one being very much a part of the other. First, it is to help mankind. And second, it helps do this from a detached viewpoint, for astrology is objective. It is also important to understand that on a personal level objectivity is impossible. Only when something is viewed impersonally can any real truth be ascertained. The things most personal to each of us are our values, our ideas, concepts and principles that we hold dear. We also value our ability to create in accordance with our own unique identity, and our unconscious sexual longings. These things are symbolized by the second, fifth and eighth houses, which form two squares and an opposition to the eleventh house. This eleventh house has often been called the house of dreams, and dreams are nearly always associated with romance. Yet, this house forms a direct opposition to the fifth house of romance. Thus, there is an apparent paradox that makes the eleventh house difficult to understand. To find its real meaning we first have to see how this house completes a grand cross with three other houses that all involve specifically deep commitments. What an individual values in his second house, he is willing to fight for. The romantic interludes of his fifth house keep him deeply involved on a most intimate level. And, the unconscious sexuality of his eighth house represent perhaps the most deeply intimate involvement of all. With all of this, an individual needs what one might call "a way out." In essence, it can be likened to the valve on a pressure cooker. In all the experiences that require commitments or involvments where we must stand for something, we endure pressure from others. For the sake of sanity there must be some place in the horoscope that represents a way of momentarily breaking the intensity of these commitments, so we can free the spirit and renew energies. The only way a person can do this is to be impersonal, aloof, detached, or disinterested in what is going on round him.

We can do this through the eleventh house. When sexual attachment becomes too intense, we can experience an impersonal consciousness through this house. The sign on the cusp of the eleventh shows what we have to gain by being impersonal.

The traditional dreams that the eleventh house symbolizes are what the individual is acting out when he needs to relax. He should remember that when he uses his eleventh house too much, he becomes the dream that he uses to escape from reality. Once he becomes this dream, he may have difficulty knowing the difference between the dream and reality, as happens so much with individuals who keep taking on impersonal disguises to mask what they are really seeking.

The art of being impersonal can be extremely effective when one knows how to use it and can balance it with the personal nature. But, not everybody truly understands what being impersonal means. There are literally thousands upon thousands of people following spiritual leaders who are trying to lead an impersonal life style. They are actually giving up their needs for the development of values (second house), their creative abilities (fifth house) and the biological or unconscious need for sexual expression (eighth house) in order to do this. The question arises, "Are they running to something or *from* something?" Unfortunately, in most instances they are running from something. Sad indeed is the case of spiritual disillusionment that each of these people will eventually reach when they discover they ignored themselves for the sake of another human being who will one day disappoint their ideals (because he is human). True impersonality comes from a detached consciousness and the awareness of being a part of the evolvement of the whole. This perspective develops as we come to learn to internalize the highest ideals so they become a part of our total being. As children, we are exposed to the "superhero" figures who are untainted and incorruptible. They always work for the public good. They have some unique mystical power that sets them apart from the average man. And although they are sexually attractive, they never get involved in sex. In this sense, they are unattainable. To top it off, they rarely if ever, work for money.

Think about the comic book heros that children begin their escapist fantasy life with. Heroes like Superman, Wonder Woman, Captain Marvel, Batman and Robin, etc. We have been exposed to the ideals these superheroes stand for. Regardless of how much our life fails to live up to these standards, a part of us wishes it could. Interestingly enough, the only way these superheroes could perform their amazing feats was because they were not personally involved. We know of their abilities, uniforms or tools with which they performed their miracles. We don't know much more. Their personal social existence didn't exist. They weren't looking for personal fulfillment; they did not live for personal gain. They are the future (Aquarian) ideals of the entire human race.

The eleventh house, then, appears to be in an escape from one reality as we strive to taste another. Actually, it is not an escape at all. By loosening our commitments on a personal level we are able to find a greater commitment to mankind's ideals which we symbolically represent. When this is achieved, we each on an individual basis, can begin to balance the different commitments we feel on the different levels of our being.

The fifth and eleventh house polarity represent the balance that we need to achieve between the creative expression of romantic instinct and the higher ideals which make us feel that life stands for something greater than ourselves. When the thoughts, actions and deeds of these houses are in harmony, it becomes possible to experience a tremendous sense of fulfillment in life.

Aries Fifth House—
Libra Eleventh House

With Aries in the fifth house, the individual is sowing the seeds of beginnings. To do this he must be highly independent. Love affairs make him aware of the danger of losing himself in another, and he may go to great lenghts to see that this does not happen. On a sexual level, he can be hedonistic, for his approach to the creative process tends to be primitive. His desires are many and he may be able to aggresively pursue them without considering that he hurt another person's feelings. Usually he is attracted to lovers who seem unattainable for the idea of conquest is strong in him.

Physical sexuality is a battleground for his ego. He tries to overpower his partner and may receive gratification by keeping his partner in a submissive role. As time goes by his partner may learn how to fight back. When this occurs, he may move on to new partners, because he cannot face the possibility of losing or being rejected by someone who is becoming as strong as he is. On a spiritual level he realizes that the seeds of beginnings have been successfully planted.

In the sex act itself, this placement carries a strong amount of narcissism. He has great enthusiasm and anxious anticipation, but may pay little attention to the finer nuances of sex. He focuses his mental energy on how quickly he can win another or how he can conquer that person by completing the act, and then he moves into new areas.

Through the Libra eleventh house, the individual desires the peace of mind he can only achieve by detaching himself from his desires. He has the ability to view situations from both sides, but he can do this only when he is not personally involved. The Aries fifth house often indicates that he jumps into involvements before thinking about them. Then he has to back away to see how much he has thrown himself off balance by leaping before looking. It is difficult for him to benefit from the advice of others. The tendency to leap before looking causes involvements that are too deep. To balance this, he may be impersonal about his hopes, dreams, wishes or ideals.

Both reactions are extremes. The Aries-Libra lesson must be learned firsthand. He must go through experiences which teach him that selflove and the love for others are two sides of the same coin. They complement each other in positive expression or negate each other when either one is seen negatively. In time he learns that by adhering to the ideals of peace, love, harmony and fairness, he can discover self-expression through creative love.

KEYWORDS: aggressive, tense sexual drive, impatient, cobative, seeks new challenges, sometimes bisexual, energizes partners, self-righteous, judgmental, exhibitionist tendencies, possible divorce, discovers the self through creative love, frustrated desires, extremely moralistic in later years, overly idealistic, sometimes runs from own expectations.

Taurus Fifth House— Scorpio Eleventh House

With this placement, the individual is sowing seeds of enduring substance and meaning. He has a large sexual appetite. It is not only the quality of sex that is important but also the quantity. He is a passionate lover. His ideas of creation may be more passive than active. There is the feeling that the fruits of life should come to him rather than being sought. In some measure this feeling masks rejection fears that the individual would rather not confront. He is happier being convinced of his solidity, rather than going out on a limb to test it.

The creative needs of Taurus center around building stability, security and comfort. A person with this placement looks for sexual experiences which have a sense of lasting solidity. Endurance assures him of the eternal quality of creation itself. He tends to pick sex partners who are either highly insecure or who are going through limbo phases in life. His quality of enduring sustenence is of value to those who believe things don't last. His natural warmth and tenderness are important to those who missed such qualities in childhood.

The person with the Taurus fifth has a tendency to get stuck on the personal level. He may stay in a love affair long after he knows the "glow" has gone. By using the detached, aloof, clinical impersonality of the Scorpio eleventh house he can learn how to end love affairs when they are over. He can learn to move on to new things rather than wallowing in what may not be worth preserving.

The imaginary heroes at the core of his foundation are always strong and righteous. When he learns to be impersonal, he can get in touch with this part of himself. In this impersonal state of consciousness he can ruthlessly cut away the sham of society that binds him to old habits which are not longer useful. He is a most sincere crusader, willing to fight and die for what he believes.

The Taurus-Scorpio polarity symbolizes the struggle between the constructive and destructive forces in life. This individual needs to learn how to build on love so he can create a solid future. At the same time, he must also be completely willing to discard all the false ideas that are obstructions to his evolution. The expectations of Scorpio are high, causing unrest and discontent. The placid comfort of creative love expressed through the Taurus fifth house is a part of his life goal. When the individual balances these two signs, love is transformed by the ideals of Scorpio and this transformation insures its endurance.

KEYWORDS: sensuous, natural warmth, excess, future promise, passionate, possessive, jealous, seeks commitment, self-indulgent, reformative, volatile changes to create harmony, obsessive love making, sensitive, intuitive, demanding, regenerates the ideals of creative love.

Gemini Fifth House—
Sagittarius Eleventh House

With Gemini in the fifth house, the individual is sowing seeds of understanding. The ideas that come through love become more important than physical sexual expression. Creation involves words, thoughts, and flirtations. Gemini is the mimic and needs models to follow, people to imitate and concepts to act out. This individual creates by copying the thought streams of others. Usually he shows a keen interest in sexual literature, and likes to hear stories of other people's love adventures. This makes him feel that he is somehow participating in their lives while still remaining within the safety of his own cacoon. The sign Gemini is ruled by Mercury, and tends to be underdeveloped on a sexual level. Platonic love, friendships, companionships, and relationships which are kept on a superficial level are more comfortable. Anything that requires a deep commitment is difficult for the Gemini to handle.

Gemini is the sign of understanding. In love matters, the person with a Gemini fifth house will try to see himself in his own role, but also through the ideas he believes his partner values. He sometimes falls in love with ideas rather than a person. Should the lover change his values the reason for the love no longer exists.

The Gemini fifth house often indicates one who derives pleasure from mental voyeurism. This may occur as a form of escape from the realistic intensity of thoughts and ideas that occur through intimate love relationships. When too many conflicting thoughts make him feel confined, he tries to escape from the confusion. He tries to expand his life through the Sagittarius eleventh house. In this part of the horoscope he can become philosophically detached and protect himself. This tends to make him sexually cold, capable of experiencing "one-night stands" or meaningless encounters that enable him to retain a sense of freedom.

Both signs lack warmth, closeness and the intimacy possible with a lover. Whether personal or impersonal, he loves ideas, words, thoughts, thought patterns, philosophies, principles, and mental constructs. Rather than being sincerely in love the *idea* of loving is what manifests through the Gemini fifth house. The Sagittarius eleventh is impersonally restless. It symbolizes the desire to dream of romantic far away places, foreign interludes or untried horizons. Both Gemini and Sagittarius have a flighty quality that makes them inconstant. These signs need a domineering mate so that the ever-pouring stream of consciousness can be directed toward a constructive outlet.

The lesson here is to combine ideals of higher mind with the actions that stem from lower mind thoughts. The individual with this polarity needs to choose lovers who can reason or who are creative. The true happiness of this polarity comes when the individual realizes that love is a teaching and learning experience through which both partners unfold.

KEYWORDS: inconstant, flirtatious, coy, curiosity-seeking, interest in sexual literature, game-playing, sometimes frigid, plays roles, extremely active mentality, over-idealistic, kind, thoughtful, lowers the sex drive, frustration from incomplete experiences, voyeuristic, cold, needs mental stimulation, philosophical, dependent, insincere relationships, great observatorial powers, legal difficulities through love, truth seeker.

Cancer Fifth House—
Capricorn Eleventh House

With Cancer in the fifth house, the individual is sowing the seeds of emotion through his warm and affectionate love nature. The person seeks honesty in his sexual relationships so that he can have a feeling of building more security as time goes on. He tries to seek a partner that he can nuture. He must trust someone before he will allow himself to feel love.

Perhaps more than any other sign, this placement indicates an individual who desires to do things that increase the comfort and security of the person he loves. On a sexual level, he is highly emotional and romantic, although somewhat conventional. He is attracted to people who will accept his mothering instinct. He can give to those who feel unprotected in life's "jungle." Cancer is the sign that rules memory. This individual will teach his lover how to go back into the past, picking up pieces of overlooked security which are extremely important for the future.

The Capricorn eleventh house creates an ideal of martyrdom. On an impersonal level, the individual believes that the greatest use of one's life is to dedicate it to something that will outlast it. When he loves on a personal level, he is constantly nourishing his partner. If he gets emotionally exhausted from this, he runs to his Capricorn eleventh house to cool off. Although he can be extremely warm and loving on a personal level, he can hide his emotions when he has to. The sensitivity of the Cancer fifth house often needs protective buffers to keep from getting hurt.

The Cancer-Capricorn axis needs loyalty and devotion from a mate in order to sustain the chronological continuity that these two signs represent. Relationships that start and stop, do not encourage the security that this individual needs to develop. Capricorn is a demanding sign. Its ideals of steadfastness and endurance can only manifest when the emotions of Cancer are expressed. The risk of being sexually vulnerable is strongly related to the expectations of future safety.

The lesson of this placement is to combine the warm, nurturing and nourishing love of Cancer with the quality of enduring ideals that Capricorn will accept. When this is achieved, love and purpose, sex and meaning, nourishment and achievement all can be blended into a powerful lasting quality of great value.

KEYWORDS: sensitive, creative, honest lover, possessive, masterful, attentive, ability to overcome obstacles, sensuous, possible Oedipal conflict, struggle with emotions, shy, sincere, dependable, long lasting affairs, strong attachments, extremely giving, must develop trust, seeks closeness, must overcome inhibitions, protective, nurturing, easily hurt, romantic.

Leo Fifth House— Aquarius Eleventh House

The fifth house is the natural placement for Leo, sign of love and romantic adventure. Here the individual is sowing the seeds of creation. He is highly sexed and proud of it. More than any other sign, he will bring out the talents, abilities, and creative instincts in his lovers. His love nature is possessive and jealous, which he may justify because of what he has to offer. He feels there is no logical reason for the person he loves to need anyone else. Being extremely ardent in his affections and often generous to a fault, he also demands much in return.

There is a powerful molding effect here as the Leo individual tries to bring his lover to a better lifestyle, a higher level of living and a more positive outlook on things in general. Sexually, he enjoys daring his partner and goading the other person into things he knows represent either fear or inhibitions. The reason he does this is to strengthen the power of the Self in the person he loves.

Through the Aquarius eleventh house, the individual experiences the most natural blending of his ideals with his reality. This is the ruling placement for Aquarius, and as a result, the individual's imagination is able to break established barriers and peer far into the future. When he is able to detach himself and look at things from an objective distance, he can dispassionately understand his place in all that is going on around him. He knows that things can be different without necessarily being better or worse than another, but he can only live this kind of a consciousness when he is truly impersonal.

The Leo-Aquarius polarity symbolizes struggles with will-power. Willpower, however, is not really a singular dimension. Aquarius symbolizes the will and Leo represents the power. When both the will and the power of an individual are harmonious it becomes possible for the person to direct life.

Although this is a ruling placement, the individual's love life is never really easy. He must use willpower to add meaning, purpose, and direction to his relationships. Only when he does this, can he find the fulfillment he is looking for.

The bravado of Leo coupled with the desire for uniqueness of the Aquarius eleventh house sometimes manifests itself in exhibitionist tendencies, for this person has a great need for an audience. He wants to show that he is fearless. He needs the respect of his mate in order to respect himself. He must also maintain a position of leadership in any intimate relationship.

The lesson here is that fulfillment is only possible when the power of love overcomes the love of power. It is one thing to want to crusade for another in an attempt to lead them to a better life. It is still another to allow the power of sincere love to guide and direct one's creative instincts, dreams, and ideals. When this is done, any negative expressions of this polarity have a miraculous way of disappearing and in their place the true expression of love, sex, and love for one's impersonal self in a world too large to ever understand completely, takes over.

KEYWORDS: autonomous nature, highly creative, inspirational, sharp, aggressive love-making, demands loyalty, proud, fair, giving nature, acts out romantic roles, powerful will, daring, brazen, open, sometimes exhibitionist tendencies, flamboyant relationships, exaggerates passions, futuristic ideals, hidden interest in orgies, strives for unique expression, sees love as a challenge, high standards, narcissism, finds creative power through love.

Virgo Fifth House— Pisces Eleventh House

With this placement the individual is trying to sow the seeds of "perfected love." Although he may be attracted to many people, he can instantly perceive who is wrong for him or what is unchangeable. In order to be happy he must be highly selective in choosing his mate.

In some instances, his ideals are so high that the expected behavior pattern often works in reverse. Realizing the impossibility of ever reaching an ideal of perfection in an imperfect world, the individual may decide to be non-selective, maintaining the attitude that in the long run it really doesn't matter anyway. When this attitude pervades a person's thinking, it can lead to periods of promiscuity.

In his physical sex life there is a desire to keep things on a light level. During the deepest moments of raw lust, he never seems to be more than innocently experimenting in order to feel as "grown-up" as he believes others are. It is interesting to note that this individual is highly conscious of what others think of him. He puts boundaries on his sexual expression, dividing into computerized parts all that he is able to label in his mind as being either good or bad. Both the male and female with Virgo in the Fifth house may not have to experience complete intercourse to gain fulfillment from sex. In fact, there is a tendency to want to stop at some point short of intercourse in order to preserve very delicate emotions that the individual feels might be lost through complete union with another person. He usually picks lovers who dissipate themselves by having too many scattered desires, or who have a generally lax attitude about personal hygiene.

The ideals of the Pisces eleventh are geared towards serving another through creative love. Sensual, artistic, romantic, feelings couple with the subtlety of a cosmic reality to make the dream of the idealized love nature. There is a peculiar conflict here inasmuch as the individual is a highly imaginative lover when he is not in love. Once he becomes deeply involved with someone, he forgets how he feels and begins to confine himself to the point that he cannot appreciate the intimacy and joy of personal love. There is no individual in the entire zodiac more capable of giving more than the person with this Virgo-Pisces polarity. Sensitive and compassionate, kind and delicately thoughtful, this person usually attracts lovers whose volatile nature only he can understand. Love often becomes a crusade for decency and spiritual truth. Periods of sexual frigidity may occur on and off through the life which are the result of emotional and psychic disillusionment that the reality of life is something less than the saint-like ideals in the unconscious. At times there are tendencies to be childlike and timid. At other times powerful deep emotions go unexpressed. This occurs because the expectations of love are on a very high level.

The lesson of this placement is that all in life is mind over matter. The distance between Virgo and Pisces covers a vast area of man's understanding. The power of thought is the creative force that moves the universe. The Virgo fifth house symbolizes the way love is as we think. At the same time, the Pisces eleventh house shows how our ideals are a product of the imagination. When thought and imagination are blended into the positive channel of creative love, there is a great deal that one can experience.

KEYWORDS: idealistic love nature, sensitive, seeks perfect love, vast imagination, compassionate giving nature, inspirational, demanding, discriminating, self-sacrificing, understanding, seeks refined pleasures, sees mate's potential, nervous love affairs, sometimes masochistic, need for loyalty, incomplete sexual experiences, organizes lovers.

Libra Fifth House— Aries Eleventh House

With this placement the individual is sowing the seeds of harmony. The art form of love in its proper balance takes precedence over everything else. There is a special delicacy to the love nature that is not found with any other sign in this house. The individual can be self-sacrificing, gentle, extremely giving, and in many ways wrap his entire existence around the person he cares for. He will identify with each relationship, wanting his partner and himself to be as "one." In this sense, he feels that half of himself is somehow missing everytime he is not in the physical presence of the one he loves. His basic lack of confidence needs constant reassurance. As a result, his dependencies tend to bring out the dominant qualities of strength in his lover. He is unconsciously masochistic and will often stay in love relationships long after he knows they are not good for him. The reason for this is that he has difficulty making personal decisions for fear of hurting another's feelings. It is easier for him to turn things around and hurt himself instead.

Basically, he is in love with love. And, when love prospers, he is the happiest and most fulfilled person in the world. Sexually, he tends to be on the submissive side, caring more for the needs of his partner than his own.

The Aries eleventh house symbolizes the idealization of oneness that the person can achieve when he is not afraid to impersonally assert himself. Getting overly intimate in love affairs seems to split this individual in half, but the more detached he can be from things, the more he is able to know the decisiveness of his own mind.

Childhood heroes are revered for their self-sufficiency. In real life, the individual does not achieve this quality, so he may try to become self-sufficient through a love relationship. After a time, he discovers, however, that sexual commitments or deep involvements are truly difficult for him. They do not lead him to self-sufficiency. Instead, his ideals become suppressed because of his need to please his partner.

The lesson here is to balance the ideals of the ego with the need for a close blending with another. Self-sacrifice, and self-assertion become the two ends of the seesaw that this individual finds himself riding on. To know when to lead, when to follow, and when to share, is the great wisdom that can be gained through this placement.

KEYWORDS: sensitive, musical, creative, alternating dominant and submissive tendencies, needs attention, tries to balance sexual partner, competitive relationships, extremes of expression, prone to flatter, ego problems, exaggerating nature, can be flirtatious, need to be soothing.

Scorpio Fifth House—
Taurus Eleventh House

With Scorpio in the fifth house, the individual is sowing the seeds of sex—the very essence of life itself. He is keen, sharp, intense and always probing into everything that is a mystery to him. He will not quit until he has the answers he is looking for. He needs to express his sexuality in the raw, crude forms that he feels in his unconscious for this puts him in touch with the very roots of his existence.

Intensely curious, he becomes jealous when he hears of others enjoying sexual experiences that he does not know. It is difficult for a mate to keep up with him, for he is in constant touch with the source of human creation. Herein lies his power, and through it, he tries to be sure that no one can outdo him.

With this placement, there is a tendency to be destructive. Love affairs can end in disaster if the individual achieves what he wants and then allows it to lose value in his eyes. Ideally, the Taurus eleventh house symbolizes the need to preserve everything. The possessiveness of Taurus, coupled with the ideals of Scorpio, often results in the inability to conserve what this individual wants most.

Through a strongly determined fixed nature, close relationships often become overbearingly intimate for others to endure. Constant transformations keep occurring through a great deal of volatile sexual activity. The individual tends to pressure his lovers to change. As a result, he often pushes them when he doesn't mean to.

The ideals of the Taurus eleventh house center around peaceful coexistence. The individual wants to establish the assurance of a calm and steady future. He knows this is not possible without first clearing away all obstacles that might act as possible sources of stagnation. He works at love, building his relationships through Plutonian transformations that he causes to occur on very deep unconscious levels. He will fight for peace because he wants it so much. Once the fighting has started he will forget the altruistic reasons why it began.

The lesson here is that the peace and love in the present moment are more important than trying to willfuly create a future that only God is certain of.* When this is kept in mind, all that is created as a

---

*Martin Schulman, *Karmic Astrology, Vol. 4, The Karma of the Now* (York Beach, ME: Samuel Weiser, 1978).

result of sex can easily blossom into enduring love. To help this all the individual has to do is stand out of the way and allow God to perform the miracles he is seeking. If he learns how to expect nothing, he will discover that through the transmutation of the sex drive he can have everything.

KEYWORDS: intense, passionate, perverse, curious, investigative, jealous, possessive nature must be transformed, instinctual, intuitive, sensitive, powerful, understands divine union of creation, can be domineering, sometimes unconsciously sadistic, protective ideals, seeks endurance through positive change, crude sexuality, demanding, psychic relationships, sex karma, must overcome destructive tendencies, regenerative relationships, creativity through transmutation of the sex drive.

Sagittarius Fifth House— Gemini Eleventh House

With Sagittarius in the fifth house, the individual is sowing the seeds of abundance. He goes through much effort to create a free lifestyle. Not wanting commitments, he is happy to know that others may want to make a commitment to him. He has a tendency to love a double standard.

He equates sex with the outdoors; associating it either with the woods, the beach or in any country-like setting where he can feel that he is blending in with the natural surroundings. He is not always faithful, for his roaming instinct is too strong for him to feel bound. His sex drive is spontaneous. He tends to get bored with the same lover.

The effect he has on his sexual partner is that of being a messenger, transmitting to her either verbally or telepathically, the precious information that guides the higher mind to truth. At least one time in the life there will be an attraction to a foreigner, or a very important love affair that occurs a great distance from home. Love and all creativity must have movement for this person is a nomad. The mind is forever moving through childhood lessons that come from nursery rhymes, fairy tales and stories which portray relationships between people and the lessons we learn.

The Gemini eleventh house idealistically desires understanding. The individual is able to see that there are two sides to everything which do not necessarily agree with each other. His peculiar fascination with life is to forever discover new dualities which show him the essence of a double universe. The more he learns about this the more he wants to learn. In fact, his thirst for knowledge is so great that he often puts it above his romantic needs.

On a sexual level, he tends to vascillate between wanting too much or wanting to avoid sex completely. Psychologically, this is an "approach-avoidance" placement. Most of this occurs because the individual's ideals are not truly his own, but rather a mixture of what he picks up from the many people in his life. The individual may experience periods of asexuality for Gemini is the sign of Platonic or non-sexual love. In fact, it is easier for this person to understand himself when he is not too sexually involved.

These two signs of mind in the fifth and eleventh houses show an affinity for understanding the creative process. It is not so much what the individual does in his love life that matters as much as what he thinks of his actions and feelings. As a result, the lessons he learns through love and sex are less physically oriented than they are directed to his consciousness. Love is the highest form of creation and with Sagittarius in the fifth, the presence of spiritual truth can become a firm foundation for the humanistic understanding that the Gemini eleventh house seeks.

KEYWORDS: overdoer, adventurer, impatient, free lifestyle, wanders, needs honesty in lovers, attracted to travel and foreign experiences, sexual messenger, exaggerates romantic needs, popular, wild spirit, inconstant, dazzling effect on others, agressive, thrives on mental stimulation, strong ego, spontaneous attractions, divorce likely, colorful romantic life.

Capricorn Fifth House— Cancer Eleventh House

With Capricorn in the fifth house, the individual is sowing the seeds of conservation so that he can preserve what is of lasting future value. His love relationships are extremely important to him. In this sense, he would rather experience something that builds slowly than a passionate affair that burns out quickly. Since prestige, honor and dignity are what he seeks, there is a tendency for him to attract people who are either rich or famous or on the verge of becoming status symbols.

His sexual patterns are both traditional and unusual. Even though he might be extremely inhibited, he nevertheless needs to maintain control of each relationship. The word "surrender" does not exist in his dictionary. Nor is he spontaneous. Instead he handles his romantic life by turning his sexual moods on or off according to his plan. There is always a method and goal behind his behavior. He tries to create form and structure in love affairs so that they ultimately build into the solid treasure he is seeking. Knowing that there are millions of people in the world that he could love, he seeks out the one who will be able to offer him the most.

He will spend time in an effort to mold his partner. By doing this, he is able to fulfill the nurturing needs of his Cancer eleventh house. However, he still has serious psychological obstacles to overcome. In his most personal intimate affairs, he holds himself back and does not readily open up to the other person. Even when he tries to detach himself and be impersonal, the Cancerian emotionality tends to bind him. Many with this placement are able to achieve their ideal by adhering to a widespread movement, whether it be founded on spiritual principles, or otherwise, so that they feel a sense of belonging to a world family. In this way, they can be impersonal and still feel the sense of protection that a surrogate-family environment affords.

On a sexual level, emotional difficulties need to be overcome. The individual needs to find a home within himself, based on whatever principle he believes is important to stand for. Only by being highly selective about his sexual partners, each of whom must stand for the protective idealized "home" he is seeking, can he realize the full value of this placement.

The lesson here is that the individual's emotional ideals can only be reached through experiencing sexuality with purpose, love with reason, and life with meaning.

KEYWORDS: attracted to important people, unconsciously ashamed of sexual feelings, sometimes inhibited, slow to form deep attachments, builds solid relationships, seeks mature reason in lovers, must balance excess motion through practicality, secretive, timid, unconscious sexual guilt, Oedipal conflicts, many emotional struggles, second half of life is easier, methodical expression, planned love nature, gives what is of greatest meaning to lover, responsible, capable of rich lasting feelings, slow to blossom.

Aquarius Fifth House— Leo Eleventh House

With this placement, the individual is sowing the seeds of the future through impersonal love. He tends to be erratic and unpredictable. His ability to remain detached from his lover can leave his mate feeling frustrated and misunderstood. He is a tremendous giver although he seldom gives what his partner wants, but rather what his instincts tell him his partner needs.

On a sexual level, he can be strangely unique or bisexual as part of his experimentally scientific instinct. He is extremely curious and if he doesn't have strongly inhibiting factors in his life, he will try things just to see what they feel like. Needing a great deal of mental stimulation to create from, he will have the fondest feelings for those individuals who supply him with knowledge. His love affairs always represent a learning experience.

He molds his lovers towards individualistic expression. Most people have an idea of what goes together and what doesn't. They match up colors, ideas, philosophies and feelings according to the way they were raised as children. After experiencing a relationship with an individual who has Aquarius in the fifth house, many of these ideas will be replaced by a new understanding.

This polarity is difficult in the fifth-eleventh house because each sign is opposite its ruling position. Although the Aquarian instincts for creativity are unhampered by the fetters of social mores, there is a lack of constancy and warmth in the love nature. Through the Leo eleventh house, the individual has grandiose ideals. He can be a difficult person to get along with for one never knows how he means what he says or when he is about to change his mind. He is extremely romantic and giving when a commitment is not required, but tends to put himself philosophically above a relationship when he has the opportunity to experience a deeply intimate involvement.

In some cases, there is a chauvinistic attitude about sexuality coming from the fact that both Leo and Aquarius symbolize struggles with the will. Whenever the individual feels that a sexual relationship is starting to own him, he will find ways of wriggling out of it only to dream of a lasting fulfilling sexual relationship. He is capable of running from what he wants to dream about it rather than experiencing it. He does act it out with those who do not demand a commitment. In that way he can give love and still remain detached from the reality of the situation.

Trying to be free from that which is intimate, coupled with the strong attachment to intangible ideals causes much frustration for the individual. He must learn to accept the fact that ideals can be formed for the growth of the personal self, but the true experience of love carries with it many twists and turns of fate. The reality of intimate personal involvement requires tolerance. The ideals of love never really change. When a traveler realizes that the road he travels never really changes the vehicle of ideas and principles in which he rides, the journey through love and all of the sexual lessons involved in it become much easier to understand.

KEYWORDS: curious sexual nature, future-oriented, unique, strange experiences, sometimes bi-sexual instincts, strong willfull nature, crusades in relationships, expanded awareness through love, uncomfortable with binding commitments, sometimes latent homosexual tendencies, capable of impersonal love, individualistic psychological structure, super ego problems, sexually experimental, bizarre unexpected experiences, contrary rebellious nature, nosy, kinky instincts, inspirational romances, tends to live ahead of time, exciting experiences.

Pisces Fifth House—
Virgo Eleventh House

Here the individual is sowing the seeds of Divine Love. He is one of the most cosmic people in the zodiac, thriving on the dream of mystical romantic interludes. Unquestionably this person is one of the most sensitive lovers. Compassionate, kind, gentle, yet deeply mysterious, he has tremendous magnetism that is beyond verbal expression. In fact, during actual love relationships, this person says more when he does not speak; for he has a way of intuitively communicating his feelings on a level that one cannot readily see.

The molding effect of the fifth house goes through a strange reversal here. What this person actually creates for the partner is the ability to transcend molds, forms, rules. He supports his partners new concepts of feeling because it makes him more complete.

Sexually he is a highly imaginative lover, creating fantasies of other times and places that seem more real than the present reality. Unfortunately, the uniquely mystical experiences that this individual offers often go misunderstood. He appears to be loose when he is not. His morals are not easily understood by others. It is because of this that love affairs are confusing to him. Through Virgo in the eleventh he can objectively crystallize what he cannot see when he is intimately involved with another. He seeks a spiritual union which he can not always verbalize to another for in essence it is a spiritual union that he seeks. He vascillates between his desire for romance and his feelings of frustration because the romance he wants interferes with his mental clarity. He tends to live in alternating patterns of much sexuality followed by periods of self-imposed celibacy. In this way he tries to rebuild all that he gives through romantic involvement. The Virgo eleventh house acts as a breather between love affairs that drain him.

Platonic friendships with the opposite sex tend to rejuvenate him, for when he is intimately personal he grows too sensitive. When he is less personal, he strengthens his thinking body, desenitizes his psychic center, and is able to feel realistically grounded.

KEYWORDS: deeply mystical, in touch with Divine Love, imaginative, sensitive, highly creative, sacrificial, sensuous, giving, elusive romances, dissolutionment, misunderstood, gentle, self-defeating ego, can see own illusions, tries to achieve deep communication through sexuality, karmic romantic life, a seeker, difficult relationships give insight.

10. The Sixth and Twelfth Houses

The sixth house has never been looked at in terms of its influence on sexuality. Traditionally it has been said to symbolize health, working conditions, relationships with superiors and inferiors and one's sense of obligations to others. To understand the sexual meaning of this house, we must first consider that it is the natural house of Mercury's rulership of Virgo. As such, it is the area in the horoscope where an individual seeks a mental understanding of how things work.

The sixth house is where one tries to order the circumstances of life as well as understand how he is expected to deal with them. It is from feeling that there is order in life that an individual starts to sense the meaning of his finite existence.

There are different philosophical schools of thought which often argue whether a person is or is not a product of his deeds and actions. On different levels both philosophies are true. The sixth house symbolizes our deeds. What a person thinks of himself is strongly influenced by what he does do and what he does not do.

On a sexual level, individuals spend some time fulfilling themselves as well as time pleasing others. This desire to please is a manifestation of obligation that the sixth house represents. In all sexual relationships, there is an interplay between physically doing what one believes his partner expects of him and at the same time expecting his partner to reciprocate. This sense of obligation, depending upon how strong it is, creates the kind of responsibilities that a person feels he must meet. Through this house an individual learns about responsibility. When this is seen on a sexual level, it is one of the factors that adds fulfillment to the physical act. Sex without obligation or responsibility to the partner or to one's self is empty and toneless.

The sixth house rules our work. Many people who do not experience fulfillment from the sexual side of life or feel that sex dissipates too much energy sublimate those desires into work. If the individual is aware of what he is doing it will help him to cope with this sublimation. In some people, sex uses up the desire for creative output in other areas and they become lazy. In others, it makes them want to work more, as a means of balancing out the energy flow.

The sixth house also rules the physical body. Long periods of celibacy cause tensions in the body that have to released in some other way. Too much sex can deplete the body of its energy, and on an emotional level this tends to make the individual very selfconscious. Physically and emotionally gratifying sexual experiences that are in proportion to an individual's reality help the body harmonize itself as it experiences its own acceptance. The sixth house can be considered a key to sexual and emotional health by learning how to balance the sexual needs and deeds with feelings of obligation to others and to the self.

Where the sixth house rules personal perception and use of the body, the twelfth house is the ruler of the consciousness. The word consciousness can be considered a derivative of the two words, conscious and conscience. When these two words are put together, we have the term "conscious conscience," which ultimately becomes the foundation of one's consciousness. To understand this, we must consider how the conscience works.

The conscience is that mechanism within us that is capable of telling us the nature of our truth. Some people go through life making compromises with the conscience. When the conscience is distorted, the knowledge of truth becomes repressed in the unconscious. To be conscious means to be aware of all that is flowing through one's perceptions. When we live our lives with fear, guilt, shame or doubt we tend to put blinders on what we are perceiving. Our perceptions become limited, which leads us to formulate opinions and attitudes and draw conclusions from incomplete data. We distort our thinking. When we are ready to be more receptive to what we perceive, we start on the path of becoming conscious.

It has been said that there are basically two types of people in the world. There are those who know and those who do not. Those who do not know are living their lives in an unconscious state. Those who know try to open up the consciousness by living their lives with a conscious conscience.

There are few things that can make an individual experience more guilt than sex. Psychiatrists and psychologists spend years trying to help patients confront the twelfth house consciousness. For those who do not know, the twelfth house symbolizes the unconscious plane; for those who do know, this house is the proving ground for the superconscious. When the conscience is straight and clear, an individual is not afraid to be who he is. It is only from this point that the process we call evolvement can begin.

The twelfth house symbolizes the understanding that comes from the soul. The soul is only as free as one's consciousness. In the sixth house the deeds and use of the body prevade the conscious mind. In the twelfth house, the individual has an opportunity to see the complete truth of his entire being. What we do in life is important, but, what we think and know of what we do is even more important.

Our ability to change and grow must come from the inner self. When the body and personality are aware of the soul it becomes possible for the entire being to function in harmony with itself.

Sex is a part of life that can either take a person away from himself or bring him to the soul. It penetrates deep through every sub layer of the unconscious, cutting away the sham of false appearances. When an individual is honest about his sexuality, he is able to rise above the emotions of the ego that keep weakening him. The sixth and twelfth house polarity symbolize how well an individual can blend the finite reality he lives in with the infinite reality that his inner self is conscious of. Sex can be only that which fulfills the needs of the body or it can be something much more spiritually mystical that somehow touches the music inside the soul.

Aries Sixth House—
Libra Twelfth House

With Aries in the sixth house, the individual experiences both physical and mental tension about his sexuality. He often turns this into competitive work energy. Although the need for romance as a part of sex is felt constantly, the fact that sex partners do not always permit spontaneous expression makes it easy for him to justify sublimation. He is conscious of his reputation and is sensitive to situations in which he is feeling used. Aries, which is so conscious of its self-identity, spends mental energy pondering over these kinds of thought patterns.

The sex drive is instinctual. When sex is not easily obtainable or only available in forms that displease him then he must redirect his energy. Because of the physical frustration that this kind of sublimation causes, he brings a certain amount of overt or covert anger to his work situation. He will express this by wanting to dominate others in order to compensate for what he unconsciously feels is being denied him on a sexual level. With this placement, the individual's sense of obligation always relates back to himself.

The unconscious energy symbolized by the Libra twelfth house is one that might be termed peaceful coexistence. He can give silently to others without asking for anything in return. Much of this giving is accomplished through secret love affairs. The more he tries to reform others the more he develops a feeling that he is balancing himself. Most people find him a curious puzzle, for this placement is usually accompanied with Scorpio in the first. Without looking deep (which he usually does not allow), others cannot possibly imagine the gentleness of this soul. He consciously uses sex (sometimes in its most lustful ways) in order to reach people on deeper levels with the love he has to give.

The lesson here is to balance the desires of the body with the love that is in the soul.

KEYWORDS: active vitality, very sexual, over concern with physical appearance, sexually self-conscious, competitive, seeks tranquility through love affairs, misunderstood, crusader instinct, strong conflict between reforming personality and tranquil soul, nervous aggressive energy, needs cooperative mate, extremism, must overcome selfishness, hides frustrations, seeks spontaneous expression, reaching for inner harmony.

Taurus Sixth House— Scorpio Twelfth House

Here sex is an important part of the basic make up. The need for physical expression of love is often carried into work situations. Sometimes this leads to romantic affairs on the job. This sign always has a tendency to "play close to home" and as a result, this person may not gain the esteem from his co-workers, peers, or friends that he unconsciously is crying out for. If he feels the slightest bit of love from another person, he tends to outdo himself, going out of his way to be sure that he has secured the affection he needs. Often he confuses obligations with love, believing that his relationships with others have more meaning than they do. Underneath it all he knows the truth. He just puts things on such a physical level that it is difficult for him to see the forest for the trees.

He experiences much unconscious turmoil. Because he is unsettled, restless, with a drive for inner transformation, it is difficult for him to take life lightly. The volatile quality of the Scorpio twelfth house tends to make him "unseat" power that he sees in others. Somehow this underlying motivational instinct enables him to get in touch with the power within himself.

Secretly, he tends to see nearly everything on a sexual level. He is the one individual in the zodiac that is hypnotized by phallic symbols everywhere. Candles, oranges, pillows, fountain pens, nearly everything he perceives gives him unconscious stimulation. Often he does not realize this, but it is the reason why he is so emotionally unsettled. Perhaps his greatest problem is that he does not usually express his unconscious drives. Instead, they remain deep dark secrets within him, while the outward manifestations of his sexual urges are somewhat limited by his conscious need for discretion in order to protect his reputation.

There is, however, a great gift coming from this position that is more unique than any other zodiacal placement. This individual has the ability to bring other people right to their roots almost instantaneously, by getting them to realize the inner sexuality and confronting their secret motivations.*

With this polarity the body needs a great deal of physical touching in order for it to feel secure. Outwardly there is a strong need to express and receive love within the confines of what society will sanction. Inwardly, the soul is constantly transforming. It needs to use sex as the fuel for these transformations. The lesson here is to learn how to transform the inner self through sexual responsibility.

KEYWORDS: must achieve sexual honesty, second marriage likely, powerful soul, much inner frustration, physical need for touching, sensitive, keen perception, individualistic, tendency to overdo, possessive, must overcome jealousy, feels obligations of love, seeks mystical union.

Gemini Sixth House— Sagittarius Twelfth House

With Gemini in the sixth house sex is kept in a delicate balance. This individual can be highly flirtatious at work but is still able to separate work from play. Although he separates love and his job, he enjoys sexual jokes and is extremely curious about the affairs of his co-workers while remaining detached.

He is preoccupied with maintaining his image, and does not want to have it tarnished by idle gossip among peers and co-workers. There are two sides to Gemini. This individual is an extremist and here in the sixth house of superiors and inferiors, he sees himself as both.

Sexual temptation creates a great deal of nervous energy which he usually works off through verbal expression when he is not able to experience sex physically. The greatest conflict is that he is always

---

*This placement indicates sexual karma. See Martin Schulman, *Karmic Astrology, Vol. 1, The Moon's Nodes and Reincarnation* (York Beach, ME: Samuel Weiser, 1975): 29-32.

questioning who is gaining and who is losing during the sex act itself. Ultimately he must realize that sex is not a battle, but rather a more intimate form of communication that can say what words cannot. When he sees this, he will realize that his dharma is to learn to communicate in his relationships.

He thrives on stimulating people, experiencing a great deal of popularity through the people he meets at work. On a mundane level, social intercourse presents him with constant challenges through which he establishes his mental identity.

Through his Sagittarius twelfth house, this person experiences an unconscious need for freedom at all costs. From his very core, he desires a life of non-involvement. He does not like to make promises. The unconscious is spontaneous and is the true source of the vivacious quality that filters down through the Gemini intellect.

The Sagittarius energy is from the higher mind. This can bring him in touch with a great deal of truth if he is willing to explore his consciousness. When he does, he discovers he does not gain anything by forming relationships built on dependencies. Such relationships make him lose the feeling he has of being a free spirit inside.

The Gemini-Sagittarius polarity symbolizes obligations in relationships with others. Sex may be more of an idea than a physical manifestation. It is not what the individual does or refrains from doing that makes him what he is as much as it is what he thinks of himself. His actions and his consciousness may be at odds with each other, for he is going through a learning process. Being highly curious, he wants to know all that will satisfy mental hunger in his soul. Attractions to stimulating individuals give him the feeling that he is growing. A series of questions and answers sift through his consciousness creating one transformation after another. He can easily outgrow his partner because of the tremendous storehouse of knowledge and wisdom that he accumulates through life.

The lesson here is to mentally understand the needs of the body in relation to the wisdom of the soul. When the individual can do this, he can balance the extreme mental activity of the inner self with the way he relates to the outer world.

KEYWORDS: extreme nervous tension, need for social intercourse, must balance distance between self and others, curious nature, inwardly expansive while being outwardly restrictive, ego difficulties, must resolve role dualities, exaggerated sexual ideas, voyeuristic nature, sometimes masochistic tendencies, can be cold, must overcome self-rejection, fear of being dominated, must have freedom in relationships.

Cancer Sixth House— Capricorn Twelfth House

With Cancer in the sixth house, the individual feels a strong protective instinct that leads him to mother or smother the people he loves. Trying to sense his partner's needs with the hope that he is capable of fulfilling them, he likes to play a servant role. Through a funny psychological twist this strengthens his ego and makes him feel more powerful. On a sexual level, he will cater to his partner as long as he feels involved in an enduring relationship. Emotions play a role here as he must establish trust in an individual before he will be open. Until he can reach that point, he hides within himself.

Always attracted to someone he can build with, he seeks partners who have strong capabilities but who need a protective mothering kind of love around them. In work situations he tries to create a friendly cozy atmosphere, as co-workers take on roles of different family members in his eyes. Because this occurs on a deep psychological level, he has to be careful of these attractions at work. Without realizing it, his need to make fellow employees into surrogate family members can cause a conflict involving psychological incest every time he experiences a sexual attraction.

Through his Capricorn twelfth house, he secretly takes life very seriously. He may appear open and carefree, but that is not what he feels. Everything must have a meaning, a purpose, a goal or be directed toward an accomplishment that will help establish an inner sense of security. In this sense he is unconsciously a dependent personality until he understands what security is all about. He must learn that the only thing he really has is himself. Then his unconscious energy for achieving can flow. This gift is transmitted to others who are close to him. On a sexual level, he is careful not to melt or fully blend with another for that would mean tearing down the walls he has struggled so long to build.

He is extremely sensitive to others while inwardly knowing that he doesn't have to be. This causes a conflict which is resolved only by subjugating his emotions to the knowing of his soul. He is extremely service conscious, but it is always because he really has his mind on some inner mission that is greater than himself. The preservation of those close to him, his society, his civilization are the primary concern of his soul.

On a personal level, inner feelings of deprivation keep motivating the lower self, and there is a greater need to subjugate the self to more personal deprivation for the benefit of some greater goodness. The spiritual lesson of this polarity is to learn how to nourish others through sincere love and affection without expecting personal reward for doing it. When this is achieved, the individual can begin to understand his emotional nature within the framework of a much larger context that has greater significance for him.

KEYWORDS: nourishing sense of obligation, attracted to individuals who need inner building, suppression, attachments formed through work, sensitive to others, insecure about body, possessive marriage, mature soul, moralistic nature, compassionate peers, habitual emotional responses perpetuated to establish security, sometimes bondage consciousness, extremely sensitive breasts in the female, goal-directed emotions, need for inner boundaries, can be puritanically judgemental, strong inner defenses, builds ego through marriage, powerful mate, may have past sexual guilt, crystallized consciousness must open through emotional expression.

Leo Sixth House— Aquarius Twelfth House

With Leo in the sixth house, the individual feels an obligation to create for others. He has high expectations of co-workers as well as lovers and feels that he must help meet the potential he sees in them. This allows him to justify his own superiority by comparison. On a sexual level, he demands loyalty from anyone he loves. Even the mild flirtations of his loved one make him feel that his position is being threatened. When devotion and loyalty are assured, he is quick to reward his partner in all ways possible so as to condition such positive behavior patterning for the future. This indicates that he may see his lover as a possession rather than a person.

Usually there is a double standard, for with the demands made on his lover, he himself can be the "office flirt." He doesn't mean all that much by it, but often does this as a way of fulfilling a need for status.

The sixth house symbolizes service and Leo has a tendency to serve himself by picking a lover who enhances his ego, promotes his career, or lives up to his expectations based on pride and accomplishment. In order to fulfill his obligation to help a lover become more creative, he acts as a source of inspiration. His basic possessiveness creates a difficult spiritual lesson. He must ultimately realize that if he throws a person a fish, he is feeding that person for a day, but if he teaches his loved one how to fish for herself, he has inspired the person for a lifetime.

Much of the outer displays of ego coming from the Leo sixth house are a facade trying to hide an inner shakiness of an Aquarian soul trying to find identity. On very deep levels he experiences mood swings that might be termed anywhere from irrational to complete schizophrenia. The inner center is constantly in a state of flux, making it difficult for him to handle the ever-changing winds that blow him in many directions. He feels a strong inner loneliness, almost as if he is an outsider to all he wants to be part of. His unconscious energy is one of complete independence which forces the loneliness.

He has a difficult illusion to see through. He must learn to identify with his Aquarian cosmic self, detached from things, rather than trying to clutch and cling to people and relationships that offer him no stability.

When he accepts the fact that stability might not be what he needs, he will find that he has it in a surprising way.

Although this polarity gives the appearance of egocentric behavior, the individual is really a true humanitarian. He will give himself to whatever he feels is worthy, or to whoever stands for a worthy cause. It is this flow of people with worthy causes that motivates him to experience the instability he complains about. He must realize that he is a giver, and on an unconscious level may be far ahead of his time. The ideas that come out of his twelfth house might be acceptable to humanity twenty or fifty years later when he will be vibrating to another calling. He may be living more of a cosmic existence than a personal one. His gifts of understanding are so great that they are not really meant for any one individual, but rather for mankind as a whole, for he is a disseminator of ideas.

This is a misunderstood placement. The Leo sixth makes the individual appear to be constantly fighting battles for superiority. On a sexual level there may even be exhibitionist tendencies as a means of manifesting pride. The desire to command others is an expression of what the soul is really doing. Qualities of bossiness or insistence are always for the good of another. When this is misunderstood, relationships can cause a great deal of friction. The unconscious crusading instinct can often offend the very people that the individual is crusading for. The lesson of this polarity is to learn to tone down the intensity of one's personal power in order to make it easier to reach others. Leo symbolizes the power of the ego while Aquarius represents the impersonal ego of mankind as a whole. For this individual to achieve happiness, the demands made on a loved one must always be part of a greater and universal unselfishness.

KEYWORDS: inspirational, protective, domineering, feels obligated to create for another, inner feelings of loneliness, hidden bi-sexual tendencies, crusader instinct, need to establish honor, in tune with universal love, seeks character through marriage, ahead of his time, misunderstood, strong humanitarian nature, difficulty in marriage.

Virgo Sixth House—
Pisces Twelfth House

Virgo is in its natural placement when found in the sixth house. The individual is able to order his obligation to others so that it never throws him off center. He draws boundaries between himself and those he loves so that he can clearly see the different functions between what he does and what others do.

He likes to be self-contained, for this gives him security. He is possessive of the work he does, for his work is a definite sublimation of his personal sex drive. In this sense, he does not like to confuse his sexual needs with others. If there is anything difficult for him to tolerate it is confusion, and he will go to great lengths to order his relationships with others into neatly compartmentalized departments in his mind so that any given moment he can easily recognize who symbolizes what.

Any sexual inhibitions he may have come from his fear of

allowing others to disturb the established order that he tries to keep in life. There is a time and place for everything, and he feels it is important to keep his sexuality in the bedroom. At the same time, he likes to study others in order to improve his own sexual experiences.

The Pisces twelfth house makes him unusually sensitive. His unconscious is like a gentle cloud of love, billowing and flowing endlessly. A kind of compassionate musical poem is always moving through his soul causing him to seek out those who he can help. He can actually impersonate the unconscious energies of others, showing them the form and direction of their imagination. His own sexual imagination tends to be unusually vivid. Through his Virgo sixth house he has an unusually keen nervous system which tends to be particularly sensitive to the most minute sexual thoughts. Through his Pisces twelfth house, he is a dreamer, a romanticist, a poet bard of times gone past; and sometimes seems very much like a Don Quixote chasing the windmills that are always tunring in his mind.

He may outwardly appear selfish when he is one of the strongest humanitarians of the zodiac. His actions are ruled by his thoughts, while his consciousness is ruled by his imagination. When he is able to blend these two together, he learns that life is very much as he makes it. The jittery nervousness that he feels when he is too close to people usually stems from childhood complexes caused by a need to over-please.

On a sexual level, this polarity tends to overidealize. The individual is clean and hygiene-conscious to a fault. Sometimes this results in hypochondriachal complaints which can inhibit his sex drive. He will insist on perfect hygiene as a prerequisite for sexual arousal. The consciousness of the soul is much more open than this, however, and seeks the mystic union of sex as its ideal. When this polarity appears in the natural houses, the individual must learn how to blend what he senses of the greater universe with his ability to function in mundane reality. When this is seen on a sexual level, there is a tendency to want to solve all of the problems his lover has because his soul is capable of perceiving ultimate conclusions. This can sometimes be overbearing. When Aries in the first house accompanies this placement the individual tends to lead his lover rather than experiencing the cooperative sharing he really wants.

The lesson here is that the idealization of perfection one seeks in another can be realized through the intuitive interplay that develops in a relationship rather that constant harping at imperfections.

KEYWORDS: hypersensitive, idealistic, much nervous energy, intuitive, sensual, creative, hidden voyeurism, possible latent homosexuality, overconcern with etiquette, need to organize mate, deeply hidden romanticism, mystical, fear of losing self in unrealized fantasies, must overcome inferiority feelings, extremely secretive, sublimation through work, feelings of isolation and loneliness, much inner beauty, transformations through selfless actions, non-discriminating love affairs create rigidity.

Libra Sixth House— Aries Twelfth House

With this placement, the individual gives of himself. In fact, he gives so much of himself that he can actually destroy relationships by trying to do too much. Libra is the sign of balance, but it indicates an area of imbalance that the individual must learn how to correct. The person may have difficulty understanding the distance between himself and others. Either he tries to get too close to people (practically living in their auras), or he backs away when he really wants to be close. He torments himself trying to balance his relationships, and finds himself putting in much effort on behalf of others, who after benefiting from his efforts, leave him standing out in the cold.

This occurs because of an inability to balance obligations and responsibilities. He sways first one way, then another. He cheats himself by withdrawing from situations which could be of great benefit to him. He is a good advisor or counselor, but cannot understand the nature of his own intimate involvements. In this way, the unconscious selfish needs of the Aries twelfth house manifest themselves as hidden and symbolic temper tantrums. The soul itself is highly independent and in many ways rather primitive. The individual is first, last and always a loner. No matter what he tries to show in his outer self, his unconscious is a seething bed of desire.

He experiences crude and spontaneous sexual impulses which he will follow through on when the opportunity presents itself. The energy that comes from the twelfth house is that of the "warrior," and no matter how gentle he may be if Pisces is in the first, it is not gentleness he feels inside. Often, he wants to act on sexual impulses in order to prove that he knows how to conquer obstacles. He enjoys taking chances and wants to jump into situations just to see if he can win. His actions are based on unconscious impulses pushing him toward action and he seldom thinks between the impulse and the act.

The twelfth house is always deeper than the sixth and it reveals a more hidden part of the person. The gentle giving qualities of the Libra sixth house should be seen as how this individual tries to create an appearance of balance with those he feels are either inferior or superior. The fact that he can see people in these roles at all reveals the nature of how he feels inside. There is a quest and a goal to this polarity. Every time he learns that he can cooperate with others he is better able to find his identiy. On a sexual level, this means that desire is often hidden if its expression would lead to losing companionship or the harmony he needs from the person he loves. The inner self is constantly beginning new ideas, new paths, and meeting new challenges. These are meaningless unless they can be shared. This placement creates a volatile life style, but, the body can be harmonized through love and selfless service to another. In this way he is able to share his inner enthusiasm with those he loves. This is a survival placement, with many situations, circumstances, and events in life that force him to decide how much he can give and how much he has.

The sex life is sometimes crude and often highly active. Unconscious selfishness causes relationships and marriages to break as he may have a feeling that he is fighting for his existence.

The lesson here is that the need for sex (sometimes in its rawest form) must be balanced with the need for peace of mind. In the person's inner consciousness he seeks sex and needs to learn that love, harmony, and peace of mind go with it and may even be more important. The more this individual masters his desire nature, the closer he will come to reaching the oneness of mind that his soul is seeking.

KEYWORDS: strong survival need, flatterer, imbalanced desire nature, hidden aggressiveness, past life sexual karma must be overcome, seeks cooperation of others, nervous imbalance, mood changes, strong sexual unconscious, freedom loving, independent soul, destructive marriage, feels obligated to lovers, achieves balance through work, powerful transformations occur through loss of stability.

Scorpio Sixth House— Taurus Twelfth House

With Scorpio in the sixth house, the individual is extremely intense in all his relationships. He tends to be a crusader for the good of mankind and gets enraged at the amount of inhumanity that he sees. He is physically, mentally, and emotionally a person who wants to impress a sense of presence on whomever he meets. He likes to work in an area where the possibility of spontaneous sexual experience might present itself. He has many attitudes toward sex, but his outlook remains scientific and clinical. He may view his experience as a kind of research that helps him to understand who he is. Being one of the most passionate lovers, he is highly sensitive to physical stimulation. He doesn't believe in sham, and will often use sex to prove that things like superior-inferior relationships, power plays in the business world, or hypochondrical complaints are disguises for people missing out on the kind of raw "gut-level" sexuality he has to offer. Of all the placements in the zodiac he is the quickest to cut through the facades. He reduces people to the basic physical and emotional essence and is able to show them the very core of their unconscious motivation.

Through the Taurus twelfth house the individual experiences an unconscious fullness that most people find difficult to understand. He feels impulses to do whatever comes natural, instinctively avoiding anything in the world that feels "plastic." His instinctive feelings rule everything he does, so his sex pattern can stay the same for many years; he is not one whose unconscious can readily let go of the past. In his innermost self, he is a creature of love with a great deal of hidden sobriety. Because he is highly sensitive he can experience loneliness on very deep levels. Perhaps this is one of the reasons he clings to things and people after they have served a useful function in his life. His biggest problem is an almost instinctual complacency, as a result of which he usually has to force himself to move in the direction of making his desires a reality.

Once he overcomes laziness, he is able to realize that the energy that comes through him is an energy for doing, building and creating. There may be clandestine love affairs with this placement, tending to taper off as the individual grows more focused in the powerful energies of his soul. He does this by making priorities in his lifestyle. In relationships he is able to unconsciously give others a sense of inner acceptance.

Both Scorpio and Taurus are highly sexual signs. Through the sixth house the individual clinically tries to understand the effects that sex has on his physical body. He studies his sexual reactions before, during and after the sex act and tries to fit them into its understanding of physical love. The lesson here is that love coming from the soul can be expressed sexually through the body when it is not being used destructively for the purpose of gaining power.

KEYWORDS: intense, pasionate, sensitive, keenly in tune with partner's needs, inner fullness, understanding, discovers values through love affairs, pleasure-seeking, overbearing, strong instinctual needs, powerful sexual drive, over-sensitive to rejection, more than one marriage likely, seeks rich meaning to life, extremely giving soul.

Sagittarius Sixth House— Gemini Twelfth House

The individual desires a great deal of space in all he does. He doesn't like to feel that he owes things to people for such feelings bind him and restrict his need for expansion. There is a natural conflict here as Jupiter-ruled Sagittarius clashes with the Mercury rulership of the sixth house. The individual tends to overemphasize small matters and be oblivious to large ones. In his relationships with others he tries to ride on his luck and intuition, gliding through things as best as he can rather than plodding as others do.

On a sexual level he is never really sure of what he wants or needs. He may think he wants one thing, then seeks another. Usually this lack of abiltity to clearly define his needs leaves him unsatisfied. When he confuses himself, he becomes philosophical in order to avoid confronting too much intimacy. Being an overdoer by nature, he needs a mate who will check his leanings toward excess. In sexual performance he can be cold or aloof, not fully committing himself to ties or the warmth that goes with them. All the benefits that love offers threaten him for he fears losing his mental freedom. He lives a double standard—for he needs and enjoys the loyalty and devotion of his mate.

He feels an obligation to give others "truth," and he is capable of doing this. When he is close to someone he has an uncanny ability to see the "Gestalt" whole of something that normally would elude others. When the loved one cannot take his prophetic advice, he may lose patience and move on to greener pastures.

Much of the restlessness and contradictory thought he experiences comes from the Gemini twelfth house. Because of his dualistic unconscious, much of his lifestyle involves approach and avoidance. He moves toward something and away from it at the same time. He is capable of giving good ideas to others but because of his indecisiveness, he may not be able to follow through on the ideas he should use for himself. Loyalty to his partner may even be the result of indecision! The instinctual level can be superficial or timid. There may be a need to unconsciously copy people, absorbing their words and concepts into himself, so he can learn how to build his life.

A fairly pronounced inner insecurity accompanies the Gemini twelfth house, and the individual tends to exaggerate his obligations to others for he perceives them through the Sagittarius sixth. The insecurity is based on his not believing that he knows enough. He keeps trying to learn more and more from whatever sources he can.

This polarity puts the experience of relationships on a karmic level. The individual seeks to understand the roles he sees himself playing. His relationships are often exaggerated and the needs he feels he must fulfill can sometimes seem to be larger than life itself.

What may appear as an overactive sex drive may indeed be nothing more than the result of an overabundance of thoughts. Sagittarius in the sixth tends to focus the higher mind in the consciousness of the physical needs. When the person can begin to understand his cosmic relationship with himself and others through the Gemini twelfth house, the activities of the higher mind can begin to be directed through the soul rather than external sensitivities which keep causing it to overreact. The lesson of this placement is to develop an impersonal understanding of the Self so that the higher mind can direct the personality.

KEYWORDS: insecure, restless nature, karmic relationships, deep ideas, difficulty in expressing thought, intuitive, inner loneliness, feels misunderstood, sometimes unconscious bi-sexual tendencies, overly analytical, needs firm and responsible mate, idealistic, possessive romances, excessive ideas, sexually curious nature, voyeurism, exaggerates obligations.

Capricorn Sixth Hosue— Cancer Twelfth House

With Capricorn in the sixth house, the individual may experience many hypochondriachal illnesses. This is his way of calling attention to his inner emotional needs that he feels are not being recognized. He is a tremendous organizer at work, fully capable of managing the affairs of others, and seeing that everything is in its proper place. The sense of responsibility towards loved ones is stronger here than any other place in the zodiac. At the same time, he expects a great deal in return for his high standards demand much of others.

When these traits are seen on a sexual level, it is impossible for this person to love unless the loved one can live up to his expectations by showing some developmental progress. Love and sex are secondary to what one does for another and what both individuals gain as a result of relating to each other. He is senstive to rejection, but it is so well hidden that only astute perception can detect it. During the sex act, this person worries about performance and whether or not he is living up to the expectations of his partner. The slightest, most subtle non-acceptance of any sexual move he might make can turn him off to the entire experience, throwing him back into his hypochondriacal disguise. When he is sexually contented his hypochondriacal illnesses seem to disappear.

Much of this occurs because a great deal of emotionality is hidden in the Cancer twelfth house. The individual is not able to express these emotions easily. One of the ways he comes in contact with himself is through hidden love affairs. Those with this placement tend to have many in order to find themselves.

There is a tendency for a sense of desperation to run through the entire being causing unnecessary attachments, illusory dependencies, and romantic involvements with unfulfilling lovers. This is caused by the desperation of the Cancer twelfth house seeking expression. In many ways, the indiviudal is an inward coward while showing bravado in order to overcompensate.

The unconscious energy is of emotional evolution and growth. The person tries to nourish others to the point where he himself may become completely depleted. He must learn how to save some of his positive emotions for himself. The illusion symbolizes one of the strongest lessons in the zodiac. In no uncertain terms, this indivudal must learn how to master his emotions.

KEYWORDS: hypochondriacal, over-senitive, childlike imagination, highly-sexed, deeply emotional, psychic, very giving soul, strives to achieve emotional wisdom, tends to hold emotions in, powerful soul memories of past lives, inner feelings of helplessness, struggle for liberation, needs to build inner confidence, approval-seeking, possible divorce, needs constant reassurance, over-compensation, strong attachments bring disappointment, seeks meaningful relationships, lustful phases followed by repulsiveness at own baseness, ultra-sensitive to rejection, takes obligations seriously.

Aquarius Sixth House— Leo Twelfth House

With Aquarius in the sixth house the individual loves to give to others who are less fortunate than himself. He doesn't like promises which can be broken. It is easier for him to keep his sense of obligation and responsibility open or undefined than to bind himself to what he may not be able to fulfill. The sixth house is the house of service, and the individual with Aquarius here feels it is his duty to try to help the underdog. Usually he is attracted to people who are at low points in their lives or who are being unfairly treated. Through loving or experiencing sex with such an individual, he is able to fulfill his strong humanitarian instinct. His ideas about what he wants to do for others keeps changing. Sometimes he would rather be alone than to see himself enmeshed. The sexual versatility of this placement leads some individuals to experience bi-sexuality, homosexuality, mutual masturbation including the use of substitute objects, and in general a wide and varied spectrum that other signs would not even imagine. This is due to the fact that the sixth house rules the body and Aquarius is the sign of the experimentor. When the two are combined the indiviual wants to explore all the new and different ways he can heighten his sensory awarenesses. One of the most remarkable characteristics of the placement is that the obligation the individual feels to a mate is almost total, but at the same time impersonal. He can appear cool when he is not.

The Leo twelfth house gives the person an extremely powerful inner self. Unconsciously he is able to control and command the rest of his being. And, from this ability to control he is able to give creative power to others. Usually there are secret love affairs for he has to reaffirm his power. Regardless of what the rest of the chart is like, he is a positive individual, for his unconscious is stronger than any other in the zodiac. He can deal with things that others cannot. He can take control of a situation where others would run away. Power itself is an illusion he must overcome. Until he does it tends to lure him. He can see this trap in others, but he does not readily see it in himself.

This is a special placement for it symbolizes the struggle between the animal self and his humanitarian instinct. The Leo-Virgo cusp which will either appear in the twelfth or first house, symbolizes the sphinx. Half lion, and half human we see a symbol of command over our animal nature along with the beginnings of humane considera-tion. The individual must learn to use his Aquarius sixth house as the vehicle through which he fulfills his impersonal obligations. If he can gain command over his animal nature through the will of his soul, then his actions and relationships will stand for something.

The lesson of the Aquarius-Leo polarity is to learn how to be impersonally detached from too much body consciousness so we can use inner creative power to direct our entire being. When this is achieved, sex becomes a gift of divine inspiration from which the spiritual ego can emerge.

KEYWORDS: inventive, humane, generous, sometimes bi-sexual, extremely giving nature, great inner power, capable of divine love, creative inspiration for others, able to uplift loved ones, needs honor in love affairs, romantic soul, possible martyr complex, idealistic, tries to reform mate, great reservoirs of inner power, high expectations, hidden erotic nature, can be obsessional, musical, artistic, cause-oriented, must learn how to serve impersonally through creative love.

Pisces Sixth House—
Virgo Twelfth House

With Pisces in the sixth house the individual is compassionate to a fault. This is the most difficult placement for this sign as it rules the opposite house. The individual tries to mystically read into others what may not be there. He seeks infinite order to finite things. He puts more effort, emotion, and energy into his love relationships than he really has to. He works too hard and puts too much meaning in trivial things.

He questions where he fits in other people's lives. This is a manifestation of a strong, neurotic insecurity that nearly always accompanies this placement. What he does for others is usually unseen and may be unappreciated until long after he has removed himself from the picture. The thing that confuses him most stems from the fact that Pisces symbolizes service to another but the sixth house represents service to oneself. He is never really sure of whether he is doing too much or not enough for the one he loves.

When things do not go his way, he tries to evoke the sympathy of those around him through overt displays of "helplessness." He is a giving soul, highly responsive, and goes out of his way to please the person he loves. His sense of obligation is more cosmic than personal for he is learning the spiritual lesson of giving without knowing what he is giving.

Through his Virgo twelfth house, he has an unconscious that seeks purification. Inwardly he is an idealist and expects everyone to live up to his standards. This placement does not readily lend itself to secret love affairs as the individual usually experiences a strict sense of inner judgement.

The unconscious seeks order and sense out of everything it perceives in the universe. By putting limits and boundaries on all he perceives, he only sees parts of the whole.

Sometimes latent or overt homosexuality is found with this placement as the individual is trying to understand an unconscious sense of narcissism that pervades his being. The Pisces-Virgo polarity is extremely sensitive. Insecurity over right thinking tends to cause a certain amount of gullibility. Emotions become rationalized making self-confrontation difficult while an inner rigidity makes the entire process of growth and evolution difficult.

Although the individual is extremely giving, he does not really know how to receive. Thus, his relationships are one-sided as he stubbornly digits his thoughts in what appears to others to be his computerized soul. The inner self may be disgusted by sex but he needs. it. He is usually highly sexed while his soul wishes that sex didn't exist. As a result, the individual tends to lead a life of extremes. He must learn to use his fine art of discrimination to help him understand how to experience the more refined forms to sex which add to his soul's perfection.

KEYWORDS: conflict between high and low consciousness, creative, artistic, musical, seeks refinement, intolerant, judgmental, repressed, frustrated, must learn how to receive love, isolated feelings, masochistic tendencies, violates own ideals, good natured, neurotic complexes due to incorrect perspective, must refine the love nature.

Part 3

Horoscopes

11. Sample Horoscope Delineations

To better understand how the horoscope can be interpreted sexually, this chapter includes sample delineations of individuals with particular problems. Although the planets and aspects are shown, only the houses will be used in the interpretation in order to demonstrate how a person's basic sexuality can be pinpointed from houses alone. In addition, practical solutions to these problems can also be drawn from the houses.

Naturally, it is important to look at the planetary placements and aspects to see how they confirm, refine and add to what the houses indicate. But, the understanding of sexuality is such an enormous topic requiring years of study, one should not jump ahead in an attempt to fathom it all at once; for that is an impossible task. A thorough mastering of the houses will give a firm foundation upon which future knowledge can be built.

The charts included in this book are intended to show the reader how to understand the basic sexuality of an individual through the experiences of the houses. There are two important things to remember if one is to become proficient at understanding the horoscope for this purpose. First, a thorough reading of the planets, their positions and aspects will always modify what the houses say. Within the framework of the experiences that the houses describe, there is latitude for differences from one chart to another. Thus, the Neptune in Leo placement in the eighth house shown by Hefner's chart may manifest differently in another chart because of additional factors within the charts. Secondly, it is also important to understand that there are only twelve possible ascendants that all the people in the world can have. Many people who have the same ascendant also have similar house cusps. The reader should not make the mistake of inferring that because a Casanova has a Scorpio rising chart that all charts with Scorpio rising would be "Casanovas". This would be the furthest thing from the truth. Astrology does not work on this level. The actual experiences that people go through are narrowly limited by the parameters of their being. The interpretation of the kinds of possible experience that might manifest through different houses in the horoscope is much wider leaving enough room for a multitude of different experiences to fit in. The reader should understand that the charts are examples for study and that a full understanding of how the astrological houses influence sexuality can only be developed through a great deal of applied study to many different horoscopes.

Giovanni Casanova

Casanova stands as a legend for his sexual adventures. Originating from a family of actors, he was educated for the priesthood but was expelled for scandalous conduct. In turn he was preacher, abbe, alchemist, cabalist, gambler and violin player. Regardless of what career he was in, or what capital of Europe he was living in, he was most known as a sensualist, involved in one intrigue after another.

In his horoscope we find Scorpio rising. First-hand confrontations through sex would have been a very important part of his search for identity. Interestingly, he was also convicted of being a spy but was able to make a miraculous escape—two more traits common to the Scorpionic nature of his Ascendant. His basic identity was sustained by the hidden corners of life, where intrigue, lust, and nefarious dealings are relied upon for survival.

In the second house of values and resources we find Sagittarius, the sign of the free-spirit. Casanova was a roamer, fleeing though one country after another, always trying to find his place. But it was this sense of freedom that he exuded which attracted so many women to him. His "swashbuckling" attitude towards life (Sagittarius in the second house rules valued attitudes) was like a magnet to women

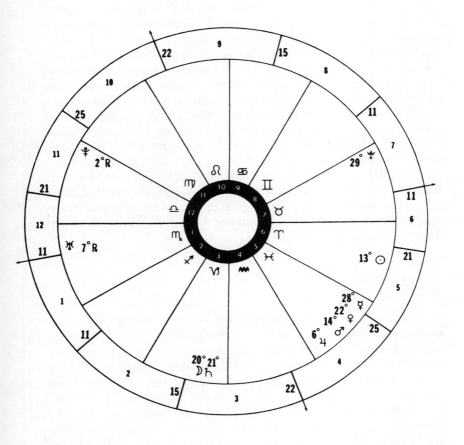

Giovanni Casanova
April 2, 1725
Venice, Italy

Birth data obtained from *An Astrological Who's Who* by Marc Penfield,
Arcane Publications, York Harbor, Maine, 1972, p. 80.

who sought freedom from the imposed restrictions in their lives. At the same time, aware that wealth and money are an important key to the freedom he sought, Casanova became director of the state lotteries in Paris and accumulated a fortune.

The third house in Capricorn shows that communication would not flow easily in his relationships. There would have to be much that he would keep hidden so as to maintain some semblance of personal dignity. He was always in the company of the great. He frequented the royal courts of Europe. He was even acquainted with the pope who bestowed a papal order on him. Thus, in his own mind (third house-Capricorn) it was important to think of himself as a prestigious individual.

Little is known of his childhood or the exact details of his formative years which would have been the roots of such an adventurous life but the Aquarius fourth house shows a sense of free-will, endless curiosity, and the spirit of adventure. He would struggle his entire life to gain command of himself, yet the very process of change which Aquarius symbolizes was the unsteady foundation he walked on. The ruler of Aquarius, Uranus, appears retrograde in Scorpio (the sign of sex) in the twelfth house (the house of clandestine love affairs). With unconscious fantasies of a power struggle deep in his imagination, the Aquarius fourth house would have propelled him to get close to some of the most regal women in Europe (Leo in the tenth house).

In all areas of life, his imagination was boundless. We can see this through the Pisces fifth house of creativity. With one sensuous adventure after another, he was basically a romanticist at heart. And yet because Neptune, the ruler of his fifth house of love affairs, appears in his seventh house of marriage, he never really sought permanent attachments. The fifth house also shows what one tries to create in another. Casanova was able to reach women through their dreams, their fantasies, and all of the Piscean illusions which separate romance from the practical mundane world. He was undoubtedly able to make women feel more beautiful, more romantic, and somehow in touch with the infinite nature of love that flows through all of us on a cosmic level.

The Aries sixth house indicates a great deal of personal tension concerning sexuality. This house rules the body and with Aries on the cusp shows a spontaneous sex drive with constant need for expression. At the same time, the individual on a physical level does not feel any attachment or loyalty to his sex partner.

With Taurus in the seventh house, we find the balance for his Scorpio Ascendant. This would show that although he was constantly experiencing upheavals and transformations, his romantic partners tended to be more consistent and loyal. In effect, he would destroy parts of himself to bring this trait out in them. Unquestionably, he left a string of unrequitted lovers all across the continent.

The Gemini eighth house shows what one receives from the sexual experience in terms of information, ideas, and the understanding of how relationships work. Gemini tends to be an inconsistent sign. Casanova sought to learn through different and varied experiences. He may have given more than he received, for the Sagittarius second house (what one gives to a sexual partner) emanates from the higher mind, while the Gemini eighth house concerns itself with the lower mind. Because of the expansive lifestyle Casanova experienced he needed to receive lower-mind viewpoints through the analytic values of sexual partners in order to maintain a balanced perspective. If we look at the ruler of the eighth house (Mercury) we find it in the Scorpio decanate of Pisces in the fifth house of romantic adventure. It would have been through sexually-acquired knowledge that Casanova was able to understand his romantic nature. The essence of romance goes beyond that of male-female encounters, for it tends to spread out to a more universal love affair that one has with the world. The way nature appears to those who can see it is a manifestation of romance on a cosmic level. The Piscean-like slipping from one countryside to another, the sliding in and out of different adventurous careers, and a continual thirst for life itself was an outgrowth of Casanova's intimate relationships and the knowledge he absorbed from them through his Gemini eighth house.

The Cancer ninth house shows an interesting paradox. Usually this placement creates rather loyal sexual attitudes. The individual seeks lasting meaning, and sees his partner as a permanent home or anchor—the nest of his feelings. In fact, this attitude is so strong that if such dependencies are not possible, there is a tendency for the individual to engage himself in worthless endeavors as emotional outlets for his frustrated feeling. In the case of Casanova, the mothering instinct in the female (Cancer) was always seen as far from home, or distantly unreachable (Cancer in the ninth house). He spent years searching for feelings that seemed to forever illude his grasp.

The Leo tenth house shows the psychological power complex through which he was attempting to establish his manhood. He would try to see himself through displays of bravado and flair. The idea of conquest (Leo) would often be turned to romance (Sun in the fifth house in Aries) as he would continually seek notoriety, wealth, power, and women to confirm his creative abilities.

Through the Virgo eleventh house he would have experienced a yearning for unreachable ideals and goals. But the opposition to the fifth house which was so strongly paramount in this chart shows how easily he could lose his goals through love affairs. There is an idealization of life with this placement which can incline one to saintly attitudes and the tendency to see others not as they are, but rather as they could be. Here, too, we find a connection with Casanova's romantic adventures. Mercury, the ruler of his eleventh house is in his fifth house of love and also rules his eighth house of sex. He would idealize the objects of his passions, making them into saintly images of his imagination. In spite of all of this, he was able to maintain enough order in his dreams and ideals (Virgo in the eleventh house) to hold his seemingly scattered life together. As he grew more impersonal in his later years, he turned his energies towards literary areas. He became a librarian (through the Virgo need for impersonal order in the eleventh house) and eventually wrote a clever but cynnical record of his rogueries and amours.

Through the Libra twelfth house we see another side to this amazing individual. In his soul, he felt the very essence of love, harmony, cooperation, and balance; all of the things he wanted to experience in the outside world. With Venus, the ruler, appearing in the last decanate of Pisces, he possessed the divine qualities of love that we often find in a nun or a monk. And it was probably this side of him that only those who knew him intimately could possibly appreciate. His soul would always be in need of harmony (Libra in the twelfth house) while his personality (Scorpio rising) kept seeking acceptance in the only places it could—the dark corners surrounding the brim of society's false pride.

Hugh Hefner, Sexual Empire Builder

In the chart of Hugh Hefner we find a Capricorn Ascendant. This is usually indicative of a strong desire to achieve something substantial in life so that the ego can be proud. Capricorn is the sign

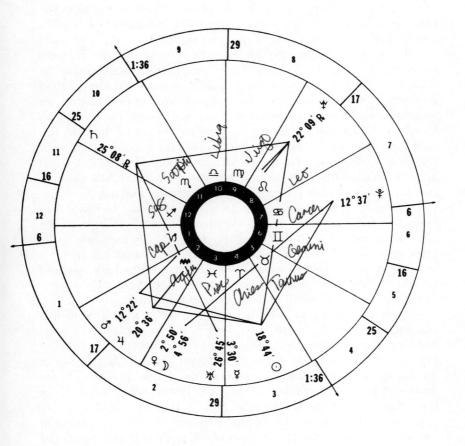

Hugh Hefner
April 9, 1926
Chicago, Illinois

Birth data obtained from *An Astrological Who's Who* by Marc Penfield, Arcane Publications, York Harbor, Maine, 1972, p. 218.

of big business, great responsibilities, and dedication toward some foreseeable goal. In the second house of resources we find the signs Aquarius and Pisces. Aquarius indicates originality, inventiveness and something that would be uniquely different from what society usually accepts. Playboy Magazine had gained its fame through its pictures. Pisces is the sign that rules pictures. The ruler of Pisces, (Neptune) is in the eighth house of sexual needs in Leo. This describes the notable Playboy centerfold that has gained its way into accepted circles. As an Aries with his Sun in the third house, Hefner would be a leader in communications. Interestingly enough, his Sun falls in the second decanate of Aries, or the Leo decanate which rules his eighth. This links the natural Scorpio rulership of the eighth with the Aries third house of communication, publishing, and disseminating information to the public. The fourth house shows the foundation at the roots of the soul in Taurus, indicating practicality, realism, a certain amount of emotional shyness, and a powerfully goal oriented life. The fifth house of creativity also starts in Taurus but then moves into Gemini. Here we see an interest in the physical pleasures through Taurus followed by the desire to communicate them through Gemini. Gemini is the sign that rules magazines and its appearance in the fifth and sixth houses shows where the creative energy would be put as well as the working conditions of life. There is a relationship coming from the sixth house back to the third house that is important. The Gemini rulership of the sixth points to the third house of communication. Both signs, Aries and Gemini, are male signs. Under the rulership of Mercury and Mars, they would symbolize the expression of a male's point of view. In this sense, Playboy Magazine tends to be a somewhat one-sided publication expressing itself through the Aries third house.

The lower hemisphere of a horoscope indicates how an individual strives to reach personal fulfillment. In Hefner's chart, we see how much he would seek to fulfill himself through his career.

Through the Cancer seventh we see that Hefner deals with others on pure emotional levels. With Leo also in this house there is a strong paternal influence in all of his intimate relationships. The eighth house which has traditionally described sexuality starts in the sign Leo. With Neptune here, a great deal of sensitive creativity would manifest. There is a need for show, flair, and display in regard to sexuality. With Virgo also following in the eighth, there is also need to achieve some ideal of sexual perfection. A standard of excellence that could somehow be related to sex would be important in order for Hefner to fulfill the criteria that Virgo demands.

In the ninth house of attitudes, we find Libra; symbolizing beauty, color, form and harmony. These interests lend themselves easily to the Scorpio tenth house which indicates a career that draws its strength from sexuality. What is particularly fascinating is the Scorpio-Sagittarius sharing of the eleventh house. Through Scorpio's sexual influence coupled with the Sagittarius drive for having fun, we see the perfect image of "the playboy" in the eleventh house of organizations, societies and clubs.

In the twelfth house which symbolizes the inner self, we find Sagittarius. Under the rulership of Jupiter which symbolizes publishing, we see the manifestation of such energies through the natural Neptune rulership of the twelfth house coming out in the form of pictures, color and higher aesthetics of natural beauty.

It is interesting to note that not all individuals know how to make use of their entire chart. With most people, houses in the chart are not being tapped. The horoscopes of famous or creative people do not follow this pattern. The successful individual learns how to use more of his potential. An individual who is using his potential experiences the houses as energies emanating from himself which are focused toward his particular sense of fulfillment. When we look at Hugh Hefner's chart, we are not surprised at how much the houses describe the career which unquestionably focuses his energies and interests.

Allegory

Once there was a man and woman who loved each other very much. In fact, their love was so deep that each saw God's perfection in the other. In each other's eyes they saw the world for their souls were as one. In each other's hearts they felt the rhythm of Divine energy for they lived and breathed as one. In each other's ears they heard the same music, but in each other's bodies they saw differences.

The sameness they felt did not need understanding, for it constantly filled them with joy. But the differneces confused them. Neither knew whose differences were better. Soon the man and woman began to grow self-conscious. Their love was unchanged, but the differences in their bodies began to make them think differently. They began to feel differently toward each other. They began to act differently. Soon the oneness they experienced with each other became clouded and obscured. The sameness that they felt was overshadowed by the differences. God's perfection was now hidden by their perception of imperfection.

The man wondered if the woman's body was truly the most perfect one he could experience. The woman wondered the same thing about the man. Soon they began to magnify the physical imperfections they saw in each other. Then they magnified emotional differences. Then they began to analyze their love for each other. In time they could hardly see their love.

The man sought other women. The woman sought other men. Each one tried to find what was missing in the other. For 12,000 years they roamed the earth. The man found many beautiful women. The woman found many handsome men. Still, in each person something seemed to be missing. As time went by, they grew weary and disappointed. Their travels made their bodies weak. Their eyes no long shone. Their hearts no longer knew what love was, for their disillusionment had brought them to despair. The ages had worn away what they thought they were looking for, and they no longer remembered.

Then one day they met. The saw each other's weary bodies, and they looked in each other's eyes. And they knew something they never knew before. No longer could they see differences between each other. Their eyes began to shine through tears of happiness. In the blurriness of shimmering truth they saw through each other's imperfections. In the humility that their journeys taught them, they were the perfection of their love. The heavens opened with mercy. The clouds of confusion were gone. And the sunlight cast its rays on the great treasure they had discovered. Their youth returned. Their weary bodies grew strong, as they became one once again. From their oneness, their love blossomed in eternal truth.